AMERICA'S HISTORIC PLACES

This first edition belongs to...

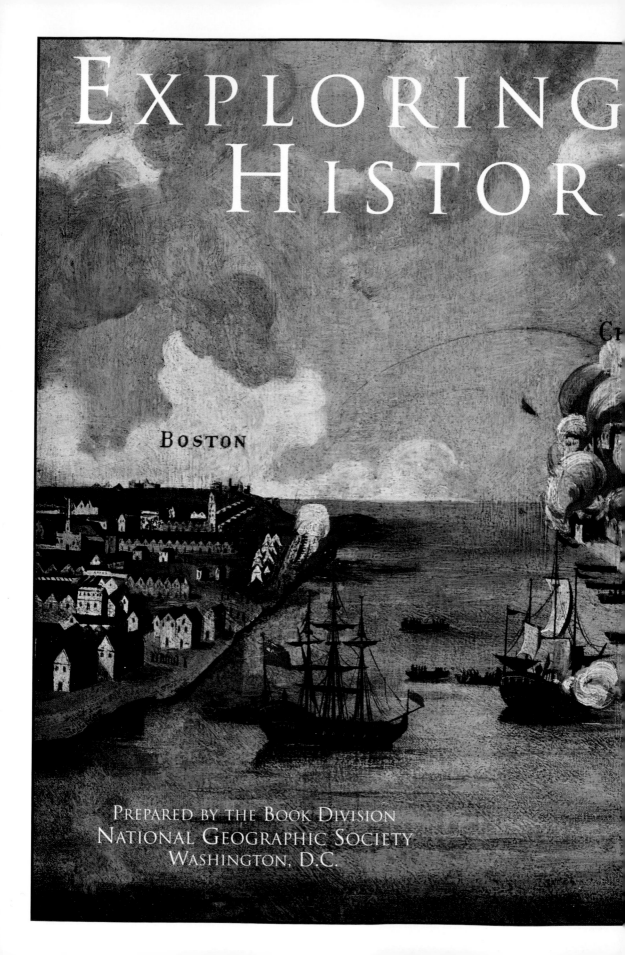

EXPLORING
HISTORY

BOSTON

CH

PREPARED BY THE BOOK DIVISION
NATIONAL GEOGRAPHIC SOCIETY
WASHINGTON, D.C.

AMERICA'S
C PLACES

Tow

Contributing Authors: Leslie Allen,
    K. M. Kostyal, and Scott Thybony

Published by
The National Geographic Society

Reg Murphy, *President and
    Chief Executive Officer*
Gilbert M. Grosvenor,
    Chairman of the Board
Nina D. Hoffman,
    Senior Vice President

Prepared by
The Book Division

William R. Gray, *Vice President and Director*
Charles Kogod, *Assistant Director*
Barbara A. Payne,
    Editorial Director and Managing Editor

Staff for this Book

Rebecca Lescaze, *Project Coordinator
    and Senior Researcher*
Toni Eugene, *Text Editor*
Mary Jenkins, *Illustrations Editor*
Suez B. Kehl, *Art Director*
Joyce B. Marshall, *Researcher*
Lewis R. Bassford, *Production
    Project Manager*
Richard S. Wain, *Production*
Meredith C. Wilcox,
    Illustrations Assistant
Kevin G. Craig, Dale-Marie Herring,
Peggy J. Purdy, *Staff Assistants*

Manufacturing and Quality Management
George V. White, *Director*
John T. Dunn, *Associate Director*
Vincent P. Ryan, *Manager*
Polly P. Tompkins, *Executive Assistant*

Anne Marie Houppert, *Indexer*

PAGE ONE: *A carriage tour ambles through
historic Savannah, whose grid of streets and
gracious squares still bears the imprint of 18th-
century town founder, James Oglethorpe.*
PRECEDING PAGES: *Smoke bellows from Breed's
Hill in this historic depiction of the 1775 Battle
of Bunker Hill. From here the ill-prepared
colonists continued their fight with one of the
mightiest powers on earth—the British
Crown—and ultimately forged a new nation.*
RIGHT: *Immortalized in art and in the minds of
Americans, George Washington symbolizes
America's finest hour. Here, early 20th-century
gallery-goers pause to admire him crossing the
Delaware River in a painting by Emanuel Leutze.*

INTRODUCTION
NATIVE AMERICANS

By K. M. Kostyal

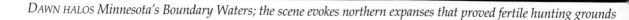

DAWN HALOS Minnesota's Boundary Waters; the scene evokes northern expanses that proved fertile hunting grounds

for wanderers who filed out of northern Asia 10,000 years ago and seeded a wealth of cultures.

F ACES OF A CONTINENT: Nez Perce, Cheyenne, Cree, Papago, and Pomo—these are just some of the native peoples portrayed in the photographs of Edward Curtis. Curtis began his monumental photographic collection at the turn of the century, recording the vanishing lifestyles of tribes that had inhabited North America for thousands of years. "The passing of every old man or woman means the passing of some

NEZ PERCE

TEWA

NAVAJO

WISHRAM

CREE

QAHATIKA

SARSI

NOATAK

CHEYENNE

POMO

tradition, some knowledge of sacred rites possessed by no other," he wrote. Decades before Curtis began his work, most Native Americans had already understood that, no matter how hard they resisted they were destined to lose both their lands and lifeways to the white settlers. "My hear is sick and sad," declared Nez Perce Chief Joseph (top row, far left) in 1877. "From where the sun now stands I will fight no more forever."

QUINAALT

WALPI

PAPAGO

UMATILLA

LUMMI

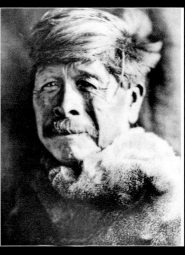

YOKUT

S OMETIME IN THE RECESSES OF PREHISTORY, many thousands of years before Europeans confidently proclaimed their "discovery" of a New World, ancient peoples arrived in America. The first colonizers wandered out of Asia, following the woolly mammoth and caribou they hunted to the eastern edge of Siberia. Once there, no impassable ocean stopped them, and they simply moved east across the land bridge that had been exposed as Ice Age ocean waters froze and lowered sea levels. When the nomadic bands reached the other side, they probably knew that they were in new territory, but the extent of it—two continents and thousands of miles in width and breadth—would have been meaningless.

Exactly when those hunter-gatherers began filtering onto the continent is unclear. Unquestionably they were here 12,000 years ago, but the nomads may have come 30,000 years before. In any case, the land they found was far different from what the later Europeans encountered, as half of North America lay buried under Pleistocene ice sheets. Some of the nomads stayed in the harsh northern reaches, others spread east and south into previously unpeopled territory. By 9000 B.C. a group had wandered as far as the tip of South America.

As the world warmed with the ending of the Ice Age, the big game the hunter-gatherers subsisted on gradually disappeared. They adapted, making new tools, discovering new edibles, becoming a little less nomadic. Somewhere in Mesoamerica agriculture arose, and the innovation spread. By 1000 B.C. the ancestral pueblo peoples of the Southwest were growing corn, squash, and beans. Their nomadic way of life gave way to settlements, and their rudimentary pit houses were

PREHISTORIC FOOTPRINT on the land, the Serpent Mound (opposite) snakes across a quarter mile of south-central Ohio. Peoples of the Hopewell Culture that flourished from about 200 B.C. to A.D. 500 left a legacy of such mounds along the Mississippi and its tributaries. Effigy Mounds National Monument (below), in Iowa, preserves almost 200 of the earthen structures, ranging in shape from a simple cylinder to the form of a bear or a bird— all presumably built for ritual purposes.

ENGRAVED SHELL GORGET
LATE MISSISSIPPIAN PERIOD
A.D. 1300-1500

BEAVER PLATFORM PIPE
MIDDLE WOODLAND PERIOD
100 B.C.-A.D. 200

COPPER REPOUSSÉ MALE PROFILE
MISSISSIPPIAN PERIOD
A.D. 1200-1350

replaced with elaborate walled pueblos. For more than two millennia the culture grew and flourished. Roads led out from the center at Chaco Canyon, threading the desert tablelands of what is now the Four Corners region of Utah, Colorado, Arizona, and New Mexico and encouraging trade. Irrigation helped ensure survival—but only as long as the rains came with some consistency. Drought constantly threatened, and at some point in the 13th century it settled relentlessly across the land. With survival threatened, fighting may have erupted between competing groups; villages were raided for food, supplies. By 1300 the people of the Four Corners region had left. Difficult living conditions may have driven them out, or a better lifestyle may have drawn them elsewhere.

To the east and north different patterns of civilization and survival had emerged. In the Pacific Northwest a coastal culture flourished on the region's bounteous sea life and immense, sheltering forests. On the capacious northern plains and in the rich woodlands that blanketed the lower eastern third of the continent, humans relied on the same three staple crops that sustained the Southwest cultures—corn, squash, and beans—and on fishing, hunting, and foraging. Gradually, Woodland Indians established a true civilization along the Mississippi and its tributaries. Later generations would call them the Mound Builders for the ambitious earthen mounds that became their trademark. Some of their cities grew to metropolises: Cahokia, on the mid-Mississippi near present-day St. Louis, boasted 40,000 residents in A.D. 1200. But, as with other cultures, drought and warfare slowly took a toll. New groups gained dominance, the balance of power shifted, the dynamic changed.

Far to the east and an ocean away, other peoples were locked in the same human conflict over territory, wealth, and power. By the end of the 15th century, these European groups had brought their conflicts to the shores of the Western Hemisphere—what to them was a New World. To their Eurocentric minds, the millions of inhabitants already there were simple "savages," who, as one historian put it, "stood as living impediments to agricultural 'civilization,' little different from stony mountains, unfordable rivers, and implacable swamps." The Europeans came equipped with cannon and musket to subdue the savages, but they unwittingly brought much more dangerous weapons than those. The diseases they carried—smallpox, measles, mumps—proved far more lethal.

On Hispaniola alone, the native population fell from a million to about five hundred just years after Columbus's landing. The same fate befell natives throughout the Americas. The Spanish conquerors, brutal and uncompromising, infected and enslaved whole populations in Mesoamerica and the Southwest, forcing them to work the land or the mines or to pay tribute.

Perhaps as a salve to their consciences, the Europeans talked of bringing the "heathen" to God, but those heathen had their own elaborate spiritual beliefs that infused the natural world with divinity.

MICA CUTOUT
MIDDLE WOODLAND
PERIOD
200 B.C.–A.D. 400

TWO-THOUSAND-YEAR-OLD *mica cutout of a bird claw and other handiwork of Woodland Indians (opposite) character-ize their regard for beauty. This complex collection of different yet connected cultures held sway in the east-ern third of North America from about 1000 B.C. to A.D. 1000. Like the Woodland Indians, their descendants— the Mississippian peoples— built ritual mounds.*

"ROCK WITH WINGS"—tse bit'a'i—*the Navajo call Ship Rock, a pinnacle that rises 1,500 feet above the Four Corners.*

Long revered, the site embodies Native American spirituality, intertwining the sacred and the natural worlds.

Animals, crops, the moon, the cycles of the seasons—all represented projections of the gods. The dynamics of native society were based on these beliefs and on the rhythms of the environment. In most tribes men hunted, fished, fought, were seminomadic. Women lived more settled lives, tending the crops, perpetuating the social fabric. To the Europeans such a division was incomprehensible. "They doe nothing but hunt and fish," one colonist complained of Indian men. In the Old World such "pastimes" belonged only to the privileged gentry. As the first tentative bands of Europeans straggled ashore along the Atlantic coastline in the 17th century, local tribes up and down the seaboard watched with curiosity and some benevolence. Not infrequently, they shared food and showed the inexperienced newcomers what crops to grow or where game could be found.

At first the incompetent white-faced aliens posed little threat. In fact, they could be exploited as allies in the more important struggle with traditional enemy tribes. And they had new commodities— metal tools and beads—to trade. As the years passed, however, Europeans poured onto the continent in a frightening flood of humanity, and it became clear that they were rapacious consumers of land, mindless in their destruction of resources, and often brutal in their tactics.

The Indians came to understand that this new "tribe" needed to be quelled. In the Chesapeake a Powhatan named Opechancanough ordered massacres of the hapless, diffuse settlers. The first uprising he led, in 1622, took almost 350 lives. The second, in 1644, was a failure, and the powerful Powhatan kingdom that had stood against the English in Virginia was defeated for all time. Within decades, few traces of the Powhatan remained.

In New England the natives and newcomers forged a less embittered relationship, but the uneasy coexistence between them broke down in the Connecticut River Valley as more and more whites encroached on the traditional territory of the Pequot. In 1637 the Indians rose up, but at great cost. In brutal retaliation, a Pequot palisade was set afire, killing hundreds of the Indians. Survivors were hunted and held captive or sold into slavery. The Pequot, too, became a lost people, but their allies remembered the egregious English attack, and the Indians of western Massachusetts would later exact retribution.

As white settlers dominated more and more land along the coast, the Indians were pushed west, shoving at other native groups and appropriating their territories. Different tribes allied themselves with different European groups. Once again the face of the land changed, and centuries-old cultures were threatened.

Even before the Europeans had arrived, an Indian prophet had foretold their approach. In a vision he had seen "men of strange appearance" coming "across the great water. I was frightened," he said, "even in my dream."

ETERNALLY ELEGANT, Cliff Palace (opposite), in Colorado's Mesa Verde National Park, survives as a triumph of Native American architecture. Leaving their traditional mesa-top pueblos about A.D. 1150, the ancestral pueblo people began to build these more protected citadels. Within a hundred years, for reasons not entirely known, the Mesa Verde people had moved south and east to pueblos along the Rio Grande River. Their descendants' stories of the spirit world are recorded in rock at Petroglyph National Monument (above), in Albuquerque, New Mexico.

CHAPTER 1
EXPLORATION &SETTLEMENT

BY K. M. KOSTYAL

BILLOWING OUT OF EUROPE, graceful Portuguese caravels revolutionized navigation with their maneuverability and

seaworthiness. Heralds of an age of exploration, they would lead the Old World to a new, undreamed-of continent.

T HE YEAR IS 1492. Across Europe the Black Death that has plagued humankind for almost a century is subsiding at last. As the population grows, the political formlessness and papal stranglehold of the Middle Ages diminish, and nation states gradually coalesce. In Portugal Prince Henry the Navigator begins pressing outward from Europe, moving boldly into the world's oceans. His engineers have invented a remarkable new vessel—the caravel—whose maneuverability, seaworthiness, and ability to sail to windward give mariners a confidence they have never possessed before. His navigators are probing the west coast of Africa and searching for new sea routes to the Orient. For 40 years land access to the riches of the East has been thwarted by the Ottoman Turk's control of Constantinople.

In Spain the year 1492 marks the demise of Islamic dominance. At long last the Moors have been driven out of Granada, their last Iberian stronghold. The decade-long campaign against

THE RIVER-WOVEN mid-Atlantic coast (opposite) seemed a land of plenty to aspiring Elizabethan entrepreneurs. By the late 16th century, Walter Raleigh's emissaries had established a tentative colony on Roanoke Island, along today's North Carolina coast. Its inhabitants mysteriously disappeared, and the English settled in 1607 on Virginia's James River. Jamestown's controversial leader, John Smith, his features set in stone (above), now enjoys unopposed command of the recently discovered site of old James Fort.

them has unified the Christian population under its Catholic monarchs—Ferdinand and Isabella—and left Spain with a strong, seasoned military. Expansive and ambitious in victory, Isabella listens as a Genoese named Cristoforo Colombo—a master mariner who has sailed for Portugal's Prince Henry—pours forth his theory that the riches of Las Indies can be had by sailing west across the Atlantic that lies at Spain's doorstep. Isabella decides to indulge the Genoese, and, in August, Columbus puts out with three ships. In October he makes landfall across the Atlantic, just as he had predicted. The Admiral of the Ocean Seas—the title Columbus assumes for himself—confidently reports to the royal court that he has "reached the Indies…," and there "found very many islands filled with people without number…." Indians he calls them and quickly enslaves them to do the bidding of the Empire. Within years disease and the cruelties of Spanish slavery have reduced the "people without number" to near extinction.

Two years after Columbus's landing, Portugal and Spain, with all the hubris of their era, sign the Treaty of Tordesillas, effectively splitting the non-Christian world between them. Portugal gets everything east of the Cape Verde Islands, off West Africa; Spain receives everything west of them. Soon enough, Spain understands that Columbus was mistaken about Las Indies, though he went to his grave insisting he had discovered them. In fact, Spain's treaty portion includes no part of the rich Orient. It's ultimately of no matter, however, because by 1519 a young conquistador named Hernán Cortés—trained, ironically, in the law—has seized control of the awesome wealth of Moctezuma's Aztec Empire. Just over a decade later, a small force led by Francisco Pizarro overruns the Inca Empire to the south, and soon the gold and silver mines of Spanish America are producing ten times the mineral wealth of all other mines in the world combined.

MESOAMERICAN GOLD (above) filled 15th-century Spanish coffers. Francisco Coronado explored the desert Southwest, finding adobe pueblos like Acoma (right) instead of the riches of the famed Seven Cities of Cibola. Acoma sprawls across a mesa west of Albuquerque, inhabited today as it has been for seven centuries.

Ever hungry for more riches, other conquistadores are pushing north. Hernando de Soto, Pizarro's deputy and a veteran of the Inca and Aztec campaigns, lands on the west coast of Florida with 600 men in 1539. For two years he wanders through Florida, crossing the Appalachian Mountains into the Tennessee River Valley to explore what is now the Carolinas, Alabama, Oklahoma, and Arkansas. Gold, jewels, any sign of the wealth of South and Central America elude him, and he dies at last on the banks of the Mississippi. During almost the same period, a 30-year-old grandee named Francisco Coronado leads an expedition north from Mexico into the Southwest and on into current-day Kansas. He is searching for the legendary Seven Cities of Cibola, but all he finds are dusty pueblos scattered across the vast spaces of the Southwest.

"Gold is most excellent," Columbus once wrote. "Gold constitutes treasure, and he who possesses it may do what he will in the world, and may so attain as to bring souls to Paradise." Decades after

Columbus set foot in the New World, his sentiments still embody Spain's approach to conquest. Not yet interested in settling new lands, the Spanish come simply to exploit wealth. Men are sent, not families, and their task is to pull mineral riches from the ground and send it back to Spain. Other European countries watch warily as Spain grows ever more rich and powerful off the largesse of the Americas. Each of these countries has its own ambitions and its own unique problems, problems that might be solved by laying a claim to this newly found and untapped hemisphere of the globe.

As early as 1497 England sends out a Venetian, John Cabot, to search for a sea passage to the Orient. Probing the northern tip of New-foundland, Cabot fails in his search, and, like other intrepid mariners, loses his life in the process. But the English, even before Cabot, have discovered the rich fishing grounds of the North Atlantic, and that lures some fishermen across the ocean, where they become familiar with the coast and the local natives. The French, too, have turned their

gaze on the New World, and, 30 years after Cabot, their explorer, Jacques Cartier, at last locates a broad body of water penetrating the northeastern end of the continent—the St. Lawrence River. It provides no northwest passage to Asia, but the St. Lawrence does eventually open a lucrative fur trade that will occupy the French for two centuries.

FAR TO THE SOUTH, in Florida, French Huguenots also attempt settlements in the 1560s and '70s, hoping to practice their new-found Protestantism in peace—and to parry Spain's consuming claims to the region. The Spanish fight hard to keep the French out—and they succeed. In 1565 the ruthless Don Pedro Menéndez de Avilés destroys the French settlement of Fort Caroline, on bluffs above the St. Johns River, and butchers its "heretics." Menéndez goes on to build a chain of posts and missions on the ruins of the failed French colony. At a deserted Indian village he establishes a headquarters settlement—St. Augustine. It is destined to reign as the oldest continuously inhabited European city in North America, and it guarantees that Florida will remain Spanish for 250 years to come.

Fanning up the Atlantic coast, Spanish expeditions reconnoiter the bountiful Chesapeake Bay, whose estuaries they find banked by

"fertile and pleasing land…a great quantity of chestnuts and large walnuts, as well as wild vines with swollen grapes." By 1570 the Spanish have established a Chesapeake mission on the banks of what will later be called the York River. Local Indians have learned of Spain's vicious treatment of Native Americans, however, and they destroy the mission within months.

As the century closes, Spanish adventurers again march into the Southwest, this time with the aim of settling there. With the ruthlessness that has come to characterize his country's imperialism, their leader, Don Juan Oñate, brutalizes the local Indians into paying tribute and sometimes laboring on Spanish estates, or *encomiendas*. Cattle and sheep ranches and small Spanish settlements like Santa Fe soon dot the endless aridity of New Mexico.

But Spain's dominion in the Americas is rapidly drawing to a close. In England, one Sir Humphrey Gilbert has received a patent from Queen Elizabeth I to "inhabit and possess…all remote and heathen lands not actually in possession of any Christian prince." After a brief reconnaissance of the North American coastline, Gilbert returns to England and begins to sell millions of New World acres to anyone who will purchase them. Setting out with a group of colonists in 1583, he is lost at sea. His half-brother, Walter Raleigh, presses the enterprise, and by 1585 his recruits establish a tentative settlement on Roanoke Island, part of the temperate but windswept world of Carolina's Outer Banks.

Meanwhile, the irrepressible British sea dog, Sir Francis Drake, is reveling in harassing and pillaging Spanish settlements and ships in the Americas. In 1587 he sails into St. Augustine harbor and burns the Spanish fort to the ground, then proceeds up the coast to check on the English group at Roanoke. Disheartened and without supplies, the

FIRST AND LAST bastion of Spanish might in Florida, the Castillo de San Marcos (opposite) has guarded the Matanzas River and St. Augustine since 1672. Even a century before the star-shaped fortress was built, this stretch of coastline was contested ground. Wresting the area from the French in 1565, the Spanish then had to guard against the English, whose cannonballs leveled St. Augustine in 1702. From the debris of battle, the Spanish resurrected their city. The oldest house (above) dates from 1727, but the site has been occupied since the early 1600s.

colonists there abandon the island and sail away with Drake. Walter Raleigh, however, will not be deterred. He soon dispatches another group of 90-some hopeful souls to Roanoke—a group that will become legend. In 1590, when supply ships from England arrive at Roanoke, they find the colony lost, abandoned. On a tree "in fayre Capitall letters was graven CROATOAN without any crosse or sign of distresse...." Trusting that the colonists have escaped hostile Indians and gone to live with a friendly tribe, the English reinforcements sail back to Europe. As long as Raleigh's settlers are considered alive, his claim to Virginia—this land where the "soile is the most plentifull, sweete, fruitfull, and wholsome of all the world..." remains intact.

England itself has become a "new world" in the closing decades of the 16th century. The old way of life, farming, has fallen prey to a growing spirit of commerce. English wool is in such demand abroad that large landowners have turned their small tenant farmers off the land and built enclosures for raising sheep. The so-called enclosure movement has uprooted thousands of farmers, and volatile bands of the poor and homeless now roam the countryside. At the same time the newly minted merchant class is searching for a way to establish a balance of trade. England needs a place to export her products as well as her surplus population.

tion. Across the Atlantic lies the answer—Virginia, the land named after the Virgin Queen, Elizabeth. "View her Lovely lookes...her Virgin portion...she is worth the wooing and loves of the best Husband," writer Samuel Purchas rhapsodizes about the New World—though he has never seen and never will see it.

In 1603 James I succeeds Elizabeth to the throne. Accusing Sir Walter Raleigh of treason, James has him imprisoned—and eventually executed. Raleigh's charter goes to a group of London merchants, though another group of merchants, based in Plymouth, also has designs on America. In 1606 King James charters the Virginia Company, dividing the land across the Atlantic between the two syndicates. Eyeing their southern portion, the London group moves quickly and within a year dispatches three ships, the *Susan Constant*, the *Godspeed*, and the *Discovery*, to establish a "plantation"—a transplantation of English society—in Virginia.

O N "THE SIX AND TWENTIETH DAY OF APRILL, about foure a clocke in the morning, wee descried the Land of Virginia…," George Percy reported. It had such "faire meddowes and goodly tall Trees, with such Fresh-waters running through the woods, as I was almost ravished at the first sight thereof…." For two weeks the band of 104 colonists feasts on wild strawberries and roasted oysters as it explores the lower Chesapeake and the broad tributary named for the English king. Percy calls the James River "one of the famousest Rivers that ever was found by any Christian…where ships of great burthen may harbour in safetie." Harboring in safety is of great concern to the English. They remember too well the unknown fate of the lost colony at Roanoke, and they know that the Spanish threat is always imminent. Finally, they choose to settle on a small island in the river, where the channel cuts so close by that they can moor their ships to trees. Ironically, in all that vast Atlantic coastline, they have chosen a site not 15 miles from the place where the Spanish established their Chesapeake mission 30 years before.

"ONE OF THE GREATEST and fayrest havens in the world," Huguenot Jean Ribaut said of the island he chose in 1562 for his Charlesfort. Depicted in a 16th-century engraving (below), the fortress gave the French a southern toehold. When food ran low, the Huguenots paddled inland to the village of Chief Ouadé for supplies (opposite).

The Virginia spring feels fresh and hopeful, with no hint of the miasmic pall that will settle over the marshy island with the arrival of summer. The colonists quickly set to work building James Fort and clearing the island's woodland to plant wheat they have brought with them. They are governed by a council of seven men appointed by the London Company. One of the seven, John Smith, has been held captive since the Atlantic crossing, apparently because he offended some of the aristocracy aboard ship. Brash, not a "gentleman," but the son of a yeoman farmer, Smith is a seasoned adventurer and soldier of fortune who has fought the Turks in Hungary. Perhaps better than any man among the colonists, he can adapt to a foreign place. Finally, on June 10 Smith is released and given his rightful seat on the council. He quickly forms liaisons with the local Powhatan Indians and begins surveying the surrounding lands.

The hopefulness of spring quickly fades as the fetid heat of a Virginia summer spreads disease through the group. Ironically, the colonists probably brought the carriers of malaria with them when they stopped in the West Indies on their way across the Atlantic and loaded mosquitoes along with supplies. As the heat drags on, foods spoil, and,

The manner of their fishing.

INHABITANTS

IN THE DECADE OF DISCOVERY AND SETTLEMENT

AN ARTIST'S HAND immortalized the life-ways of Algonquian Indians. John White, artist and governor of Walter Raleigh's doomed Roanoke colony, spent 1585 and 1586 in America before being "con-strayned to return to England." When he came back three years later, the colonists, including his granddaughter Virginia Dare—first English child born in the New World—had vanished.

White's tableaux of local Indians saved the native culture from being lost to history. In "The Manner of Their Fishing" (opposite), White painted a composite detailing different Algonquian fishing methods. Amidships in the dugout a clay-pot fire blazes to attract fish at night, while in the shallows men cast weir nets and spears. A painting of a palisaded Pomeiooc village in the tidewater of Carolina (above) details the mat- or skin-covered frame houses that

the seminomadic Algonquian used. As seasons changed, communities literally pulled up stakes and relocated to better fishing or hunting grounds. In the center of the settlement, villagers gather around a leaping bonfire.

"They solemnise their feasts in the nigt, and therefore they keepe verye great fyres to auoyde darkness," explained White, who also drew detailed sketches of the wildlife he saw on his brief sojourn in America.

PIRATICAL PANACHE characterizes legendary Elizabethan sea dog, Sir Francis Drake, in an oil portrait. Circumnavigating the globe in 1577-80, Drake reconnoitered the northwest coast of North America to near the present Canadian border. In South America and the Caribbean he played havoc with Spanish ports and treasure fleets, relentlessly burning and pillaging them. In 1588 his bold maneuvers in the North Atlantic helped defeat the Spanish Armada and end Spain's dominion on the high seas.

weakened by hunger, illness, and a lack of leadership, the group does little to ensure its own survival. By summer's end fewer than 50 colonists are alive. Struggling on, they somehow make it through winter, spring, summer. Then, the following September John Smith becomes their leader, imposing at last some plan for survival, some routine—"Those who do not work do not eat"—on the colony. To help matters further, 70 new colonists arrive in October, among them skilled workmen sent by the London Company to produce glass, pitch, and anything else that will turn a profit in Europe. After all, the financiers in London consider this toehold in the New World no more than a commercial venture, and they are chronically pushing the colonists to turn a profit. Gold is forever sought—and never found, though there is one early, false find. Timber is shipped back, wine is attempted, but no export shows any real commercial promise.

Conditions in the colony grow suddenly worse again. Injured by a gunpowder explosion, Smith is forced to return to England—as much by his rivals in the colony as by his health. The Powhatan, whose relations with Jamestown have always been uneven, turn hostile; rats, it is discovered, have eaten the stored grains. The winter of 1609-10 becomes known as the "starving time." Desperate, the English eat "dogs, cats, rats, snakes, toadstools, horsehides…even human corpses," one survivor admits. The winter proves cold and long, as the world suffers in the grip of a little ice age. When spring arrives, only 90 of the 300 colonists are left, and they have no struggle left in them. In June they sail down the James for England. Before they reach the Chesapeake, they meet a ship headed upriver with news that a well-supplied English fleet is just behind. Jamestown, it appears, is not destined to become yet another lost colony.

In 1614 relations with the Powhatan improve when a young colonist named John Rolfe marries Pocahontas, daughter of the powerful Powhatan chief. Such marriages are rare among the English, who covet their Englishness and want to perpetuate it in America. This marriage leads to the Pocahontas Peace, several welcome years of good relations between the English and the Indians. Rolfe's contribution to the colony does not end there. A committed smoker, he experiments with new tobacco strains because the native variety, *Nicotiana rustica*, is considered "poore and weake, and of a biting tast…." Using seeds imported from Trinidad, Rolfe succeeds in cultivating a better-tasting tobacco that seems eminently suited to growing conditions along the Chesapeake. Shipped to England, the Virginia tobacco has to compete with Spanish imports, but by 1617 the colony knows that at last it has found a viable export. Every available bit of settled land, even the streets and marketplace, are given over to plantings of the "esteemed weed." In a bid to attract and hold new immigrants, the Virginia Company finally allows individuals to own their own land instead of working plots for the company.

After a decade of hardship, the English toehold in the New World has grown to a foothold, as new plantations have spread along the James, and settlers have become "seasoned"—able to withstand the diseases and bacteria of the New World. The Chesapeake colony is no longer an experiment, and the agrarian way of life that will mark it, for better or for worse, during the next 250 years, is already well established.

The same year that the London Company sent out its first colonists, the Plymouth Company dispatched its own employees to the coast of what is now Maine. The group, under the leadership of George Popham, erected a fort at the mouth of the Kennebec River and labored to build a pinnace, the *Virginia*, out of the splendid Maine timber. The ruthless winter proved too much for the settlers, and in less than a year, they abandoned the site. It will take more than just commercial ambition to conquer the harsh New England conditions. It will take religious zeal. In the Europe of the early 17th century, that zeal is in great abundance.

THE CENTURY BEFORE, A GERMAN PRIEST, Martin Luther, had attacked the spiritual hegemony of the Catholic Church and launched the Protestant Reformation. The movement gained strength with Swiss theologian John Calvin, who preached predestination and God's "election" of only certain souls to eternal paradise. Now, as the 17th century unfolds, England vacillates back and forth between Catholicism and Protestantism, depending upon the current monarch's own beliefs. Among the Protestant Anglicans there are those who want to "purify" the church—Puritans, they are somewhat derisively called. More "radical" zealots want to separate from the church completely. Persecuted in England, one such group of Separatists escapes to Holland in 1608, but by 1620 they begin to chafe at the idea of their children becoming more Dutch than English. Petitioning the Virginia Company, they receive permission and some funds to settle in America. In September 1620, a small ship, the *Mayflower*, embarks from Plymouth, England, crammed with supplies, 35 committed "saints," and 67 "strangers."

Probably these ardent souls, "who knew they were pilgrims," hoped to settle at the mouth of the Hudson River. The area had been known in Europe for a decade, ever since English navigator Henry Hudson explored it for the Dutch in 1609. But the *Mayflower*'s course wanders north, and in mid-November her passengers at last spy the tip of Cape Cod. With winter threatening, they will have to make do with this area. After several weeks of searching the coastline for an appropriate place to settle, their leaders at last choose a protected coastal site named earlier by John Smith on one of his far-ranging expeditions: Plymouth, it is called. Knowing that it lies outside the London Company's acknowledged territory, the passengers sign the Mayflower Compact, establishing a government and confirming their allegiance to England's king. It is already December 21 when they disembark.

Perhaps more than any other early group, these settlers will capture the imagination of later generations of Americans. Plymouth Rock, no more than a legendary landing place identified decades after the Pilgrims' arrival by one of their descendants, will be enshrined, literally, in a small marble temple. More than just another group of colonists, or "Old Comers," as the passengers later call themselves, these settlers from the *Mayflower* become immortalized as the Pilgrims, their struggles writ large in the national psyche. *(continued on page 36)*

NOW KNOWN to the world as Pocahontas—"little play thing"—the Indian princess Matoaka came to symbolize a bridge between two worlds. Daughter of the Chief Powhatan, friend of Jamestown's John Smith, and wife of John Rolfe, Pocahontas was Lady Rebecca to the London society she charmed on a 1616 trip to England. Struck ill as she set sail for America, she died on her way down the Thames and is buried in English soil.

(continued on page 36)

JAMESTOWN, VIRGINIA

AT JAMESTOWN SETTLEMENT thatched wattle-and-daub huts (left), and the replicas of small, 17th-century ships (above, left), re-create the early English struggles in Virginia. After exploring the Chesapeake Bay and its estuaries, the leaders of the 1607 London Company expedition settled on an island in the James, "where our shippes doe lie so neere the shoare that they are moored to the Trees...." Ill-equipped for the world they found, the colonists came laden with Elizabethan notions of class and warfare. While their chain mail suits (above) might protect them on the battlefields of Europe, such accoutrements were no help in staving off such enemies as starvation and disease.

" **T**HEY SOUNDED THE HARBOR and found it fit for shipping, and marched into the land and found divers cornfields and little running brooks, a place (as they supposed it) fit for situation." So William Bradford, long-time leader of the Pilgrims, described the group's choice of Plimoth Plantation. Today, a re-creation of the small, tidy village stands on the windswept coast of Plymouth Bay, and life goes on here as it did in the 1620s (below). God-fearing "Pilgrims"

thatch roofs (right), gather crops (opposite), brew beer, and talk of the "savages" with whom they have established an uncertain peace.

English-speaking Indian Squanto showed the Pilgrim settlers how to trap eel and plant corn, and the first fall hunting season yielded such an abundance of wildfowl that a thanksgiving seemed in order. Some 90 Wampanoags joined that celebration, contributing five deer of their own, and for three days European and Indian feasted together.

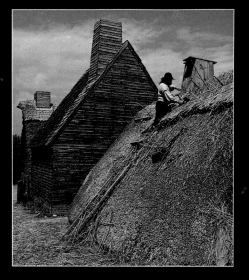

As they struggle through the 1620s, the plight of the Pilgrims must have seemed far from romantic. Like the Jamestown colonists, they endure a "starving time" during that first winter. "Wanting houses and other comforts; being infected with the scurvy and other diseases" resulting from the long sea voyage, half of them do not survive. But the remainder of the Plymouth colonists persist, and the local Wampanoag Indians provide assistance, showing them how to grow corn and gather local seafood. Their governor for 31 years, William Bradford, guides them with a steady, uplifting hand. "All great and honourable actions are accompanied with great difficulties,"

he admonishes, "and must be both enterprised and overcome with answerable courages."

Poorly supported by their London benefactors and never commercially successful, the Pilgrims' small New World settlement somehow perseveres as the faithful scratch a living from the rocky North Atlantic coastline and practice their beliefs in peace. Some of their numbers, seeking even greater religious freedom, move from Plymouth, establishing their own outposts in the wilderness.

THE PILGRIM EXAMPLE encourages other disaffected souls in England. Charles I, a Catholic monarch, has laid a heavy hand on the Puritans within the Anglican Church, and by 1630 a group of successful Puritan merchants is eyeing America longingly. The king, apparently unaware of their religious affiliation, agrees to charter them as the Massachusetts Bay Company. Far from the small fringe band that the Pilgrims had been or the commercial experiment that the Jamestown group had represented, the Puritans are well funded and well organized. In May 1629 an advance party of some 400 is dispatched. They establish a plantation fronting a harbor within the protective lee of Cape Ann, not far from Plymouth. Soon they change the area's Indian name, Naumkeag, to a Hebrew one—Salem. The following spring 17 ships bearing almost a thousand souls set sail for Salem under the unswerving leadership of Governor John Winthrop. The "Great Migration" is under way.

Trickling into Salem harbor a few ships at a time, the Puritans catch their first glimpse of the New World, but find that Salem itself, as one of them put it, "pleased us not." So they move a little south down the coast, building several settlements— Boston, Dorchester, Watertown—in the vicinity of the Charles River. As the colony slowly prospers, more and more of the disaffected follow the Great Migration across the Atlantic. By 1641, 21,000 Europeans have settled in New England—on land that once supported the Indians.

The Puritans do not welcome all comers to their ranks. They discourage the lower classes, and the ungodly. And they tolerate no dissenters. One brilliant young theologian, Roger Williams, finds himself

GAINING INDEPENDENCE from Spain in the early 17th century, the Dutch quickly joined the race to America. In 1626 Dutch colonial Governor Peter Minuit made one of history's best real estate deals when he paid Canarsie Indians the equivalent of $24 for what is now Manhattan Island. In a 1660 draft of the New Amsterdam street plan (left), the outlines of such modern landmarks as Broadway and the protective wall that would give rise to Wall Street are already in place. No wall, however, could permanently secure Dutch claims here, and by 1674 New Amsterdam had become the English settlement of New York.

BREACHING THE INTERIOR, the broad Hudson River briefly convinced its explorer, Henry Hudson, that he had

found the elusive Northwest Passage. The river and its lush valley proved fertile ground for colonization.

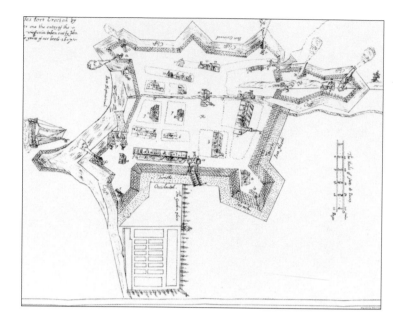

in trouble almost immediately. On his arrival in 1631, he refuses a ministry in Boston because he cannot reconcile himself to the Anglican ritual, even in the Puritan form. Accepting a post instead in Salem, Williams is soon upbraided for his radical views—that Indians should be paid for their land and that individuals can find their way to God outside the strictures of the church. Moving to Plymouth, then back to Salem, he continues to flout the strict doctrine of the Puritan fathers from his pulpit, contending that "forced worship stinks in God's nostrils." Williams's out-spokenness cannot be tolerated, and in the winter of 1635 the Puritan fathers move to banish him. Warned in advance, he flees south to Narragansett Bay and spends a winter among the Indians, surviving, apparently, by his own wise dictates: "Seek and make peace, if possible with all men" and by the same token, "Secure your own life from a revengeful, malicious arrow or hatchet." In the spring a group of his followers joins Williams on Narragansett Bay, and there they establish a settlement, Providence, whose reputation for toleration soon spreads.

A FANCIFUL EXAGGERATION depicts a 1607 English fort at the mouth of the Kennebec River as an elaborate European-style citadel. In fact, Fort St. George survived barely a year before its band of adventurers gave up in the face of the area's frigid winters. Considered part of Massachusetts throughout the colonial era, Maine settled slowly, as disaffected souls from the rigid Puritan enclaves to the south escaped north to this less constrained wilderness. The early coastal village of York got its start in the 1630s and still preserves its colonial heritage, including the 1719 gaol (opposite), one of the oldest public buildings in the country.

W ILLIAMS'S ACTIONS and those of other iconoclasts who follow his example set the stage for a gradual but sweeping sea change in the Old World mind-set. Perhaps toleration and notions of individual human choice, worth, even equality, can find a place in the vast spaces of the New World. Certainly, by the mid-17th century America's potential and wealth seem limitless, and, like the English, other nations are planting their own seeds here.

Up the wide Hudson and along the Connecticut and Delaware Rivers, the New Netherland of the Dutch is growing. Immense tracts of land have been granted to patroons, with the stipulation that they bring more Dutch families in to work them. Swedes and Finns, too, have proclaimed a New Sweden along the Delaware. And in the Chesapeake, the Lords Baltimore have received a charter for their own colony, where they hope to anchor Catholicism in the New World. The French are concentrating more on the interior, forging ties with Indians there and strengthening their fur trade. Their coureurs de bois—traders and trappers—are aggressively exploring uncharted regions of the continent.

By now all of Europe recognizes that the Old World order has shifted forever with the reality of a New World. The longtime inhabitants of the New World—the Pequot, the Powhatan, the Wampanoag, and others—know that their old order is gone forever. The next century will see these changes become more profound.

Plantations rich with the fruits of American largesse seamed the rivers of the mid-Atlantic coast in the 18th century.

CHAPTER 2
COLONIAL LIVING

BY K. M. KOSTYAL

Though balanced precariously on tobacco and slave labor, they embodied civility in the often rough colonial world.

T

THOUGH A FORMIDABLE ocean separated Europe and America, the two worlds seemed wedded to one another by fate, each twist or turn in one causing a wrench of some kind in the other. The wars and religious strife that perpetually raged in Europe found fresh ground in the colonies, affecting them in subtle and not so subtle ways. In 1642, as civil war overtook England, Puritans in New England recrossed the Atlantic to fight on the side of Oliver Cromwell's Roundheads—most of them also Puritans—and rid England of its imperious monarch, Charles I. And so the great Puritan migration to the New World ended—if only for a time.

The war in England had a wholly different effect on Virginia. In 1642 an aristocratic young royalist had taken the helm of the colony. Governor William Berkeley would lead Virginia for 35 years, and, during that time, change the face of the Old Dominion. When he arrived, the low, coastal swag of rivers and tobacco fields that characterized Virginia's settled lands was inhabited, according to one observer, by "none but those of the meanest quality and corruptest lives." The blue-blooded Berkeley quickly set about to reverse all that. Recruiting England's "distressed Cavaliers," disenfranchised by the war—and by the egregious beheading of their king—Berkeley doubled Virginia's population in his first decade, expanding it from 8,000 to 16,000 souls. He was determined that this colony, at least, preserve royalist notions of class and place. It was his "recruits"—Carters, Harrisons, Custises, Pages, Lees, and others—who would sire the dynasties destined to dominate Virginia society and politics for centuries to come.

Even now, at the end of the 20th century, their great houses rise on the wooded Virginia riverbanks, monuments to a heritage that has not quite become extinct. Along the broad, meandering James River just north of Jamestown, a cadre of these plantations—Berkeley, Shirley, Westover, Sherwood Forest, and Carter's Grove—turn their faces to the river and their backs to the inroads of the passing centuries.

Always unstable, the English political landscape reversed itself again in 1660, when the Stuarts were restored to the throne. Charles II promptly rewarded the loyalists who had fought for the monarchy with land grants in America. More farsighted than the early financial companies that had backed the first colonies, these Restoration proprietors were motivated not by quick profits but by permanent colonization. Within a decade and a half, three new colonies had been carved out of the continental wilderness: Carolina, Pennsylvania, and New York. Wrested from the Dutch, who were a growing thorn in the side of the English, the former New Netherland was renamed New York after its proprietor, the Duke of York. By the time the duke ascended the English throne in 1685, the colony, with its rich Hudson River Valley, its prosperous port of New York, and its melting-pot mix of peoples—Dutch, English, German, French, and Scandinavian—had four times as many European inhabitants as it had had when England seized it. In addition

SOLEMN SPIRIT of the early Puritans, who mistrusted worldly pleasures as temptations of the devil, pervades the austere 17th-century John Whipple House in Ipswich, Massachusetts (opposite). Though the Puritan fathers exercised an iron hand in southern New England for decades, by the 18th century their grip was slipping, and craftsmen, like Boston silversmith Paul Revere, were celebrating beauty in their finely honed pieces (above).

to contending with one another, these Europeans had to coexist with the long-established Mohawk of the Iroquois Confederacy.

Like New York, none of the new colonies was a homogeneous transplantation of English folk on American soil. Each colony had a distinctive character and had been birthed with a very specific aim in mind. Almost small countries unto themselves, the colonies developed their own cultures and economies—and their own internal strife.

In Carolina that strife was particularly pronounced. Isolated, small farmers peopled the colony's northern half, while the south, centered around the burgeoning port of Charles Town, quickly developed a flourishing commercial economy based on lumber, cattle, corn, and furs. Many of the area's wealthy planters had come from Barbados to settle the new, rich continental grants. They brought with them the African slaves who had worked their Caribbean fields—and they brought, too, entrenched notions of classism. At odds from the start with the hardscrabble farmers to the north, these wealthy southern planters had more in common with their well-heeled Virginia brethren.

As the 17th century wore on, Virginia, too, began to rely on an enslaved labor force. Until the 1670s the colony had encouraged settlement through the headright system—that is, every incoming colonist received a land grant of 50 acres as an incentive to immigrate. Those paying passage for indentured servants received an additional grant of land for each "head" they imported.

In Virginia's early decades many aspiring colonists came to the New World as indentured servants. Once their years of servitude were over, they were free to make their own way in the New World. Many became successful members of colonial society, were elected burgesses, and became landowners. Some, like carpenter-joiner William Buckland, left an indelible mark on the Chesapeake heritage. After Virginia planter and statesman George Mason brought Buckland over, the master craftsman made Mason's Gunston Hall a regal show-place. Buckland's elaborate paneling and wood trim still ornament the Potomac River plantation. Once free of his indenture, Buckland prospered as a sought-after artisan among the colonial elite. Not all former indentured servants found life in the New World so promising. Some arrived at the moment of freedom only to find themselves facing uncertainty and even destitution. Disaffected bands of them—usually young men—wandered the countryside, adding an unpredictable element to the population.

Slaves, on the other hand, offered a more predictable labor alternative. Easily controlled and in servitude forever, they could be forced to the backbreaking labor that fed the Virginia tobacco crop and the southern Carolina rice fields. Centuries before, in 1450, Pope Nicholas V had sanctioned slavery, and slave trading had long been an accepted practice in Europe. In the mid-1600s slave ships began importing Africans into the Caribbean sugar fields of the new English plantations. It required no more than a simple leap of history for slavery to cross the waters separating the Caribbean from southern Carolina and then move up the coast. Virginia's Governor Berkeley had long advocated making an industry of slavery, first suggesting a trade in Indian slaves, and, when that failed, in Africans. By the 1670s more and more Virginia planters were beginning to see slavery as an answer to their labor needs.

What was no more than a solution to a labor question for the white colonists was a decree of doom for many Africans. Once captured, tribespeople were herded into the breathless, stinking holes of slavers that usually lacked even enough headroom for a human being to sit up. The dread voyage across the Atlantic was often a fatal one. The Africans who did survive became part of one of the largest ethnic migrations to the Americas—a forced migration. By the century's end, Africans held in bondage made up 10 percent of the total colonial population—but far more than that in the South, where the system suited the stratified society the royalist planters wanted to perpetuate. "In Virginia and the Carolinas, they have a vast multitude of slaves," Englishman Edmund Burke reported to his Parliament, concluding that, "Where this is the case in any part of the world, those who are free" see their freedom "not only as an enjoyment, but a kind of rank and privilege." Once grafted onto American soil, slavery rooted itself deeply. Before it ended, more than nine million Africans would be forced from their home continent into lifelong bondage in the Caribbean and the Americas.

GEORGIAN SPLENDOR of the Governor's Palace embodies the ambitions Virginia's royal governors had for their new capital of Williamsburg. Laid out in the early 1700s, the small town served as colonial capital until the Revolution. The original Governor's Palace burned to the ground while being used as a hospital for Continental troops wounded in the Battle of Yorktown; the current replica was built on its foundations.

FAR FROM THE ELITIST NOTIONS of the Southern gentleman—both in miles and in minds—lay the Puritan ideal of the honorable man, one who was, as church father Cotton Mather expounded, "studious, humble, patient, reserved and mortified...." New England society insisted first upon godliness, and, as a corollary, in conformity to social and religious norms. Individual deviation in behavior, or even thoughts, was out of the question. Unlike the Southern colonists, who valued their space and thus spread themselves out in small and large farms that kept "troublesome neighbors at a distance," the Puritans laid out the small tidy towns that still grace the New England countryside. Soaring above the village greens were white-steepled Congregational meetinghouses. In their bare, unheated interiors church fathers held forth for hours at a time on the perils of sin and the eternities of hellfire. Often the bounty heads of wolves, their dried blood streaking the walls, looked down on the congregation like wrathful demons. A descendant of those early Puritans, Harriet Beecher Stowe, characterized their world as "one of profound,

On WILLIAMSBURG's *Duke of Gloucester Street, mobcapped shopkeepers rekindle pleasantries and hardships of*

18th-century life. Since the 1930s hundreds of the town's colonial buildings have been restored or re-created.

unutterable, and therefore unuttered, melancholy, which regarded human existence itself as a ghastly risk, and…an inconceivable misfortune."

A rigid oligarchy of elders ruled these communities of somber souls in their "sadd colors." Each town and church acted almost as an independent unit from the rest, caring for their own and relentlessly ensuring that all adhered rigorously to the doctrines of faith. Allegiance to God, family, and community was paramount, though personal industry and good business sense were also well respected. Literacy was particularly highly valued, "it being one chief project of that old deluder, Satan, to keep men from the knowledge of the scriptures…." To make certain that "Learning…not be buried in the graves of our forefathers…," Massachusetts Bay Colony law required that towns of a hundred families have a schoolhouse, and, as early as 1636, the Puritans had founded a college in Cambridge. When a young minister named John Harvard bequeathed it his estate, the college accepted the proceeds and took on his name.

Puritans reserved their godly behavior mostly for members of their own flock. Other denominations were unwelcome, and Native Americans were shown little tolerance. They had no settled towns, possessed no land tenure nor any of the redeeming civilized qualities that the European mind could understand or respect. "This savage people ruleth over many lands without title or property," proclaimed Puritan minister John Winthrop, first governor of the Massachusetts Bay Colony, "for they enclose no ground, neither have they cattle to maintain it…." Another minister intoned, perhaps with a certain wistfulness, that the Indians seemed "by right of birth, to enjoy the liberty of Wild ass colts, rendering no homage to any one whomsoever, except when they like." For their part, the Indians watched as the towns of the white interlopers "spread faster than a beargrease spot on a blanket." But more than the loss of territory threatened the northern tribes. The European presence had changed the very fabric of their lives. The Indians had come to rely heavily on the fur trade—mostly in beaver pelts—to supply them with goods they had never known before— guns, metal axes, other tools, and rum. Their reliance did not always come about randomly, but instead was part of a strategy by some English toward the Indians to "put them upon desiring a thousand things, they never dreamt of before" so that "on us they must in a manner wholly depend to have them supplied."

Decimated by newly introduced European diseases and locked in intertribal conflicts over hunting grounds that had only increased with

Rich northern waters of New England kept local fishermen busy harvesting cod, then drying and salting it at shore stations like this one in an 18th-century engraving. Even before the first settlement had been planted on New England shores, European fishermen were tapping the wealth of these waters. Once colonies were under way, enterprising souls realized they could combine the timber wealth of New England with its ocean abundance and build seafaring ships to rival any in the world.

the coming of the Europeans, the northern Indians seemed powerless to stop the European onslaught. Until 1662. At that time the Wampanoag chief Massasoit was unceremoniously summoned to the court at Plymouth for questioning. Soon thereafter he died—under circumstances the Indians found suspicious. Massasoit's role as chief passed to his son Metacomet, whose English name, King Philip, would soon strike terror into the Puritan soul.

A TOBACCO PLANTATION

By 1675 Metacomet had managed to unite tribes in the area, and for two years King Philip's War raged across eastern Massachusetts and Rhode Island. The Indians at first prevailed, fighting in the swampy bog lands with which they had long been familiar. Despite their defeats, the English stubbornly stuck to their old line-formation tactics, which the Indians found nonsensical. "English Fashion is all one Fool," one native observed, "you kill mee, mee kill you! No, better ly somewhere, and Shoot a man, and hee no see! That the best Soldier!" But such good soldiering could not withstand the combined efforts of the English and their allies, the Mohawk. Ambushing Metacomet, the Mohawk decapitated him and presented his severed head to the church leaders in Boston. One of the deadliest wars in American history in terms of the percentage of casualties it wrought, King Philip's War was over. Massachusetts had suffered serious devastation, however, and the Indian-European conflict was far from over.

T O THE SOUTH ANGLO-INDIAN CONFLICTS had exposed an even more worrisome battle for power—one between colonists and crown. In Virginia unrest with the king's representative, Governor Berkeley, and his ineffectualness in defending the colony was growing. In the 1660s, during the Second Anglo-Dutch War, Dutch warships had sailed up the James and burned a tobacco fleet lying at anchor. Settlers along the western frontier felt increasingly anxious about the Indian situation. In the spring of 1675, the situation came to a head when Doeg Indians attacked a small western outpost in Stafford County. Soon Susquehanna Indians were involved as well, and the western colonists were demanding support from Berkeley. His tepid responses did little to mollify or protect them. Instead, the settlers took hope from a newly arrived young aristocrat, Nathaniel Bacon, who stepped forward to take charge of the situation.

Cambridge-educated and related both to the prominent English thinker and statesman Francis Bacon and to Governor Berkeley, the 28-year-old Bacon had established himself on the western frontier as part

BLESSED WITH FERTILE soils and an obliging climate, the colonists of the South and the Chesapeake turned their efforts to the land. Tobacco made the great planters rich and provided a reasonable living to the far more numerous small farmers. But tobacco proved a fickle master: Prices in European markets fluctuated wildly, and weather could make or break profits. As planters later learned, tobacco virtually ate soil, leaving fields depleted of minerals after only a few years.

SNOW-SWATHED STREETS *of Deerfield recall the less peaceful Massachusetts winter of 1704. Terror struck in Februa*

when a French-and-Indian raiding party burned the small northwestern outpost and brutalized its inhabitants.

DEERFIELD'S DWIGHT House bristles with the refined tastes of early 18th-century New England. Even after the 1704 attack on the town, fertile fields coaxed settlers back, and by mid-century agricultural wealth had given rise to elegant homes along Deerfield's main street.

of the growing backwater gentry. Ambitious and possessing the natural qualities of a leader, Bacon was described as "bold, active, of an inviting aspect, and powerful elocution." While the 70-year-old Berkeley equivocated, Bacon reacted daringly to Indian provocations and agreed to lead his men against the natives. Berkeley promised Bacon a commission, then reneged, and finally denounced him as a traitor.

Bacon's Rebellion was soon in full sway across Tidewater Virginia. Bacon amassed a following of some 1,300 loyal troops, many of them disenfranchised former indentured servants, and established a head-quarters at Middle Plantation, where Williamsburg would later be founded. Through the summer of 1676 Bacon's men waged a civil war against Berkeley and his supporters. Berkeley fled to the Eastern Shore, and rebels entered Jamestown and burned it to the ground.

It seemed as if Virginia might be on the road to an early revolution, but within a month dysentery had taken Bacon's life and the rebellion simply faded away—except in the tyrannical Berkeley's memory. He spent the last year of his life exacting retribution from Bacon's rebels, dying in 1677. So vindictive was the old governor that King Charles II purportedly said of him, "That old fool has hanged more men in that naked country than I did for the murder of my father."

One rebellion had been put down, but others were to come. The tide of America was slowly turning away from the old days, when autocrats, monarchs, and church laws governed men's lives. The changing times were producing strange, unsettling events. In the small New England village of Salem a bizarre epidemic was spreading, a kind of witchcraft hysteria. Among the first infected were schoolgirls, members of a group who had broken Puritan covenants by listening to the tales of sorcery told by a West Indian servant named Tituba. For reasons still unclear, the girls accused three village women of witchcraft, and other accusations soon spread like wildfire. Following the church's unequivocal edict, "Thou shalt not suffer a witch to live," the good people of Salem put 19 individuals to death and imprisoned many more before the hysteria at last faded; 35 people were executed in New England.

Historians still debate what gave rise to the crisis, though many believe that the changing tenor of the area—from an agricultural to a seaport economy—contributed to it. Then, too, witches and their dark prince, Satan, were not far-fetched concepts in the Puritan mind, but enemies as real as the godless savages were. And those savages only added to the uncertainty of life in late 17th-century Massachusetts.

Of the many Anglo-Indian skirmishes that erupted across New England in the final decades of that century, one place has come to embody that struggle above all others: the town of Deerfield. Occupying a fertile plot in the Connecticut River Valley, the settlement was England's northwesternmost enclave for decades. Though hemmed into a pocket between the Berkshires, it was unquestionably vulnerable and contested ground. Twice before, the site had witnessed tragedies. In 1664 a village of Pocumtuck Indians here had been destroyed by the Mohawk. Within a handful of years, Puritans had settled the Pocumtuck site, drawn by the rich bottomland that was, according to one settler, "the best land we have seen in this colony." The townspeople owned their own plots but worked them in common, harvesting uncommon yields of grain. The cost of such largesse, however, was great. By 1675 King Philip's War had spread west into the Connecticut River Valley. On September 1, Indians struck the Puritan village of Pocumtuck. The women and children were evacuated, but the men stayed on a couple of weeks more to harvest the summer grain. On September 18, their wagons heaped high with grain, the men of Pocumtuck moved out in a small convoy. The Indians were waiting for them. At a small stream now known as Bloody Brook, the Puritans were attacked and virtually destroyed. Again the town was abandoned.

UNPRETENTIOUS quarters in the Wells-Thorn House mark Deerfield's rugged early 18th-century years, when Puritans who had survived the French-and-Indian attack returned to resettle the village. Today, Deerfield continues to thrive as a living community.

Still, the farming potential of the land was too great a temptation, and yet another attempt to settle began anew in the 1680s. By the fall of 1703 Deerfield numbered some 260 people, but they were becoming increasingly uneasy. The governor of New York had sent word that the French and their Indian allies were headed for Deerfield and the Connecticut Valley. Small, exposed Deerfield, still the northwesternmost village in New England, was a likely target. Vigilant and wary, the townspeople left their homes and lived within the secure walls of the palisaded fort. When in the fields, men kept their muskets at the ready. Tensions eased as the cold of winter buried Massachusetts in a comforting blanket of snow. Battles rarely raged in the depths of a New England winter.

Three hundred miles away, in the colony of Canada governed by New France, a raiding party of some 200 Indians from various

AMERICA'S FIRST college, Harvard had roots deep in the colonial past. The Puritans, whose love of learning grew out of their religious beliefs, established the school in 1636, and it prospered on community donations. By the early 1700s, Yale, Princeton, and William & Mary had opened their doors as well, so "that the Youth may be piously educated in good Letters and Manners, and the Christian Faith may be propagated...." Colonial taverns, whose signboards welcomed all comers, probably engendered as much edifying debate as the halls of learned institutions.

tribes and about 50 of their French allies started south through the hyperborean stillness. In the predawn frigidity of February 29, 1704, they arrived at their destination—Deerfield. With winter as their ally, the invaders silently approached the town, and, climbing onto the snowdrifts that had piled against the palisade walls, they hoisted themselves into the fort with little effort. The suddenly roused townspeople had almost no hope of defense. Within hours 56 men, women, and children were dead. Another 109 had been taken captive, to be marched back through the snow-swept wilderness to Canada. Twenty-one of these hostages did not survive the rigors of the march. Those who did spent 20 months with the French and the Indians before they were exchanged for a pirate, Jean-Baptiste, whom the English held and the French held dear.

Not all the English captives chose to return. According to the hostages' leader, Deerfield's Reverend John Williams, the captors had worked hard to "seduce our young ones." Twenty-nine of these young ones remained unredeemed captives, choosing to stay on in Canada. One of them was Williams's daughter Eunice, who eventually married an Indian.

She, like the massacre and march, became part of Deerfield's legend. The town, amazingly, survived and thrived and continues to do so, its colonial and federal homes gracing the wide main street, and its history now integral to the tale of Puritan perseverance.

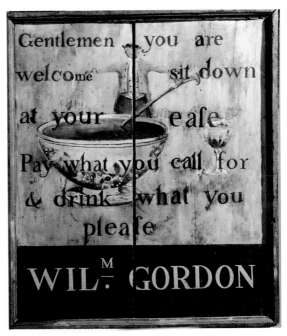

"GOD HATH MADE IT matter of Religious Exercize to my soule in getting and setling this Land," William Penn said of his colony in the New World. Pennsylvania, Charles II insisted it be called, in honor of Penn's father, a great English naval hero. In fact, it was in payment of a royal debt owed to the elder Penn that Charles granted William his colony in 1681.

With that charter Penn's Society of Friends at last had a land where they could seek, free of persecution, "that inner light," the illumination from God within each soul. For decades followers of the newfound movement had been reviled for their unorthodox spiritual beliefs, even by the Puritans, who whipped and banished Friends found on New England soil.

Only three colonies easily accepted the Quakers: Rhode Island, following Roger Williams's tradition of religious tolerance; northern Carolina; and New Jersey, where Quaker proprietors owned half the land. But the grant to William Penn opened vast new possibilities. Encompassing the tract between New York and Maryland, it took in a territory larger than the combined size of England and Wales.

Penn believed that "the world was ready for a harvest of souls that would transcend national and cultural barriers…," and this was where the harvest could begin. An astute businessman as well as an ardent Quaker, Penn also hoped to harvest (continued on page 62)

GEORGE WASHINGTON'S MOUNT VERNON

SYMBOL OF A NATION, Mount Vernon—
George Washington's estate on the
Potomac River—reflects the tastes and
times of its owner. Just as they did in Washington's lifetime, visitors flock here to appre-
ciate its grace and form.

In Washington's day guests were entertained in the formal parlor (opposite, lower);

food to feed them, prepared in a large
kitchen (opposite, top), came from the five
farms Washington owned. Though venerated
as the father of the country, Washington himself considered farming the "most delec-
table" of occupations. "It is honorable," he
declared. "It is amusing, and, with judicious
management, it is profitable."

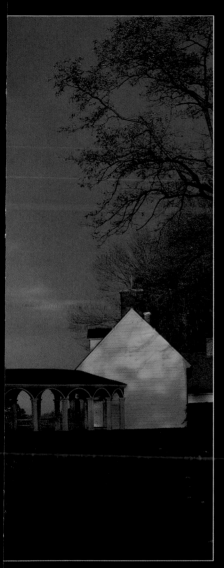

F AMILY SEAT OF AN EXCEPTIONAL CLAN,
Stratford Hall (above and opposite) was
home to the Lees of Virginia. Thomas
Lee, builder of the great house on the lower
Potomac, served as president of the colony's
royal council; his sons became ardent
patriots and members of the Continental
Congress. A later Lee destined to change
history, Robert E., also claimed Stratford
Hall as his birthplace. Lee's own mother
was born at the imposing Carter estate on
the James River, Shirley Plantation (right).
Virginia's planter dynasties often inter-
married and cultivated almost baronial lifestyles. As one British traveler observed—
perhaps ruefully—a colonial plantation
owner, backed by the labor of slaves and
indentured servants, "lives more luxuriantly
than a country gentleman in England...."

Johannes Hitchcock fecit Londini

profits from his proprietary colony. In that he was exceedingly blessed, because Pennsylvania would prove to have some of the most fertile farmland in America. Penn encouraged people from across Europe to settle on the lands of his proprietorship, and it soon ranked as the "best poor man's country."

Though the colony prospered, Penn did not. When he died in England in 1718, he had nothing material to show for his mighty endeavors. His moment of prosperity is memorialized in the rolling woodlands along the Delaware River. Restored to its former Georgian splendor, Pennsbury Manor stands again north of Philadelphia. In his heyday William Penn emerged from this palatial home to be rowed downriver to Philadelphia on a six-oared barge.

Almost from its inception, Penn's "greene Countrie Towne" thrived, quickly becoming a major American metropolis. Other port cities, too, could rival their European counterparts by the early decades of the 18th century— New York; Boston; South Carolina's Charles Town; Newport, Rhode Island: Even Maryland's newly established capital, Annapolis, once a sleepy Puritan village, was becoming an urbane mecca. Annapolis owed its charming baroque layout of radiating streets to Governor Francis Nicholson, who had designed Virginia's new capital of Williamsburg. Star-crossed Jamestown, though it had survived almost a century of colonial struggles, had never really recovered from its burning during Bacon's Rebellion. When its new capitol building was ravaged by fire again in 1698, the old island village was at last abandoned.

In NORTH TARRYTOWN, New York, the Old Dutch Reformed Church still welcomes worshipers to services. Moving up the Hudson in the 1620s, the Dutch, unlike other colonizers, made it a point to maintain friendly relations with the Native American tribes on whose lands they encroached.

A site five miles inland, Middle Plantation, was chosen for the new capital, and Governor Nicholson laid it out along a wide boulevard, with the capitol building anchoring the east end, and the new College of William & Mary, the west. At the center of town lay the Market Square, and close by it the Governor's Palace and Bruton Parish Church.

Though Williamsburg did not have the port potential to become a major metropolis, it developed into one of the few urban hubs in the state, with burgesses convening here, students strolling the streets, and tradesmen selling fine European and American wares from small shops. Life, though more provincial than in the northern cities with their mixed populations, was good in Williamsburg, particularly during the "Publick Times," when the legislature was in session and the taverns were full.

The structure of social life in colonial Virginia and much of the rest of the agricultural South, however, did not focus around cities as much as around plantations—individual farms that could range from no more than small clearings to thousands of acres. The larger plantations drove the South's class-based society, and even small farmers were dependent on the great planters to get their products to foreign markets. Virtual communities unto themselves, the big plantations were almost self-sufficient, harvesting their own lumber, making their own bricks, growing enough food to keep the great house well stocked and to feed the sometimes hundreds of enslaved humans who made the planters' lifestyle possible.

The aristocratic tradition had planted itself close to the coast even in parts of the North. In New York the old Dutch patroonships had long ago become English freehold estates, but they exercised dominion over enormous tracts of land and many lives. Philipsburg Manor, established by Frederick Philipse in the late 1600s, took in some 90,000 acres in the Hudson River Valley and acted as its own industrial-commercial complex. The adjoining Van Cortlandt Manor of Philipse's neighbor and brother-in-law covered another 86,000 acres.

BUILT FOR POSTERITY, a row of six stone houses along Huguenot Street in New Paltz, New York, now ranks as the oldest street in the country with its original houses. Fleeing persecution by France's traditionally Catholic population, French Huguenots settled here beside a tributary of the Hudson River in the 1670s.

The old Dutch patroons-turned-English-manor men were reluctant to cede any of their authority, and, when German Protestants escaping religious persecution in their homeland on the Rhine River tried to settle nearby, they were chased out by Dutch overlords. Moving south, the Germans found refuge in Pennsylvania, and became known, ironically, as the Pennsylvania Dutch. Other German refugees, among them Moravians and Mennonites, found their way to tolerant North Carolina, which had become a separate colony in 1729.

Europe's unending religious conflicts also sent a wave of Scottish Presbyterians from northern Ireland's Ulster province fleeing across the Atlantic, where they became known as the Scotch-Irish. "Tell all the poor folk...that God has opened a door for their deliverance...," one Ulsterman wrote back to Ireland. "All that a man works for is his own; and there are no revenue hounds to take it from us here; there is no one to take away yer Corn, yer Potatoes."

For all the mix of peoples and ideas in the English colonies, the crown still stood as both protector and law. And the crown meant to keep its possessions, even in the unwashed wilds of America, safe from encroachment. By the early decades of the 18th century, European settlements and forts were sprinkled across eastern North America. On the Atlantic Coast, they ran from the French villages of Newfoundland to the Floridian enclaves of the Spanish.

The English firmly held the ground in between and had extended their southern perimeter down to form a new colony—Georgia. English mili-tary hero James Oglethorpe had pushed for the colony, anxious to cre-ate a southern buffer zone abutting Spanish Florida. But he had another reason—a highly unorthodox one—for wanting his own colony. His pro-fessional duties in England had made him aware of the inhuman plight of honest debtors who had landed in prison. Why not alleviate their suffer-ing and those of other poor souls locked in the penniless despair of Old World economics by making them the farmer-soldiers of Georgia? Though few debtors, as it turned out, were released to Oglethorpe, the poor of England and the persecuted of other nations did come to help Oglethorpe make his colony a reality.

BY THE MID-18TH CENTURY, Oglethorpe's Georgia was established, and the Spanish were confined to a band along the southern sweep of the con-tinent. There, in present-day Texas and the Southwest, the inland empire of Spain was growing. Small pueblos, missions, and settlements had sprung up like mirages in the desert empti-ness, and the people were growing fat on cattle and sheep.

In the Pimería Alta, the vast tract that now takes in northern Sonora and southern Arizona, one man—Father Eusebio Francisco Kino—and his chain of missions were making great inroads with the Pima Indians, and with the geography of the West. While building his San Xavier del Bac mission, Kino noticed blue shells similar to ones he had seen on the Pacific coast. California, he became con-vinced, was not an island, as earlier explorers had thought.

Only in 1769, decades after Kino's death, did the Spanish authori-ties dispatch an expedition to what they called Alta California. The expedition's spiritual leader, Father Junípero Serra, was charged with establishing a chain of missions along the coast. At the site of his first attempts at Christianizing, the adobe facade and five-bell campanile of

the restored mission of San Diego de Alcalá gleam white in the California sun. From here, Serra spread his message north. Within a half century 20 new missions, each 50 to 75 miles apart on the King's Highway—*El Camino Real*—spanned the 500 miles from San Diego to Sonoma and spread Spanish influence west.

The French, too, had strong New World interests, but their territory was diffuse and their claims in direct opposition to the English. As the burgeoning colonies of the English seeped west into the Ohio Valley, a final contest between the two European powers became inevitable. The French needed the Ohio River system, along with their holdings on the Mississippi, to strengthen their fur trade and link their northern settlements with the French ports of New Orleans and Mobile. They had made strong allies and trading partners of many of the northern Indian tribes, which were willing to help the French press their claim. The Anglo colonists, meanwhile, were determined to settle the area themselves and to keep French expansion at bay. The settlers in the English colonies were a disparate group, however, with no unified purpose or identity save their presumed loyalty to a monarch who lay an ocean away. "Everyone cries, a union is necessary," a disgruntled colonial statesman named Benjamin Franklin wrote, "but when they come to the manner and form of the union, their weak noodles are perfectly distracted."

In the late 1740s the French began building a chain of fortresses down the Ohio Valley from what is now Erie, Pennsylvania, to the Allegheny River. For five years tensions increased as the French chased English "encroachers" out of the region. By the summer of 1754 Virginia's royal governor, Robert Dinwiddie, would have no more of it. Anxious to press his own colony's claims to the area, he dispatched an inexperienced young colonel into the valley to challenge the French. The 21-year-old George Washington and his militia then were ordered to guard a group of workmen as they erected an English fort near present-day Pittsburgh. On May 28 Washington's contingent surprised a party of French soldiers near Uniontown and successfully routed them. Knowing that word would quickly reach the French forces at Fort Duquesne (now Pittsburgh), Washington readied his men for a counterattack by hastily constructing a redoubt called Fort Necessity. To little avail. About five weeks later the expected attack occurred, taking the lives of some of Washington's men and forcing him to surrender.

THE BATTLE OF FORT NECESSITY SIGNALED the beginning of the French and Indian War. For nine years it brushed along the western border of Virginia, Pennsylvania, and New York, and pushed into Canada. In the early years Britain put little of the weight of empire behind its colonists' efforts. Then, in 1756, the Seven Years' War engaged France and England in full-scale conflict, and North America became a true theater of war. When the dust at last settled, Britain had gained almost half a continent. The 1763 Treaty of Paris awarded Great Britain all French possessions east of the Mississippi. The war had granted the colonists more than new lands on which to settle. It had also given them a taste of their own identity, as a people distinct from the British. By this time, two-thirds of the colonists were American-born, and, of the remaining third, few were British. "Fire and water are not more heterogeneous than the different colonies in North America," one observer wrote. That very heterogeneity seemed to be forging a completely new culture—indeed, a truly New World.

"In the beginning, all the World was *America*," English philosopher John Locke had written at the end of the 17th century, romanticizing the limitless freedom of a place he would never see. Yet Locke, one of the harbingers of the Age of Enlightenment, was right, and the new immigrants pouring into America, whether they knew his writings or not, seemed motivated by his novel belief that all humans were equal and by nature free to pursue "life, health, liberty, and possessions." It would take yet another conflict to codify Locke's ideals into a declaration of American liberty.

PATINA OF TIME tinges Mission San Antonio de Valero, known to history as the Alamo. In the 18th century Franciscan fathers established a chain of missions throughout the Southwest and California.

MISSIONS
OF THE
SOUTHWEST

TEXAS

"CERTAINLY, it is a pity that people so rational should have no one to teach them the Gospel, especially when the province of Texas is so large and so fertile and so fine a climate," reported a Mexican explorer in the late 1600s. Yet the Spanish made little move to settle Texas until word of French encroachments in the area spurred them to action. In 1718 Spanish friars founded the mission-presidio of San Antonio, whose simple church on the market plaza came to be called the Alamo— the Spanish word for cottonwood trees. By 1722 ten other missions had risen across present-day Texas, and in San Antonio itself four more were soon under way. Now preserved in San Antonio Missions National Historical Park, the four detail Spanish life on the Texas frontier, from the simple style of the Mission Concepción (opposite, top) to the impressively domed and ornamented Mission San José (above and opposite, lower)

A LEGACY OF IDYLLIC Spanish missions stretching from Taos, New Mexico (right), to the California coast, romanticize the often cruel reign of the Spanish Their mission-presidios stood as anchors of empire, built to proselytize—and often enslave—local Indian populations and to thwart claims by other European powers.

One hero more for the cause of religion rather than imperialism was Father Eusebio Kino, who established many of the Arizona missions. His church, San Xavier del Bac, known as the "White Dove of the Desert," was completed in 1797, and still stands outside Tucson (above).

In the 1760s Junípero Serra followed in Kino's spiritual footsteps, becoming father of the California missions. Serra based himself at the San Carlos Borromeo Mission in Carmel, where his reconstructed library (opposite) captures the simple life of a late 18th-century California missionary.

CHAPTER 3
THE REVOLUTION

BY LESLIE ALLEN

THOMAS JEFFERSON presents the adopted Declaration of Independence to Continental Congress President John

Hancock in Independence Hall's Assembly Room on July 4, 1776. John Trumbull later recorded the event in oil.

"AMERICA IS A MERE BULLY, from one end to the other, and the Bostonians by far the greatest bullies," wrote Gen. Thomas Gage, commander in chief of British forces in the New World, in late 1770. Yet those mere bullies had sorely vexed Gage ever since his regulars had disembarked, bayonets glinting, to quell Boston's riotous subjects in 1768.

To Boston's dockside toughs and ordinary laborers, the redcoated occupier was a "Lobsterback," a "damned rascally Scoundrel," or worse. British soldiers responded with insulting renditions of "Yankee Doodle," or even more insulting songs. Roving gangs brawled, and rum-fueled fistfights broke out around town; in February 1770 the killing of schoolboy Christopher Snider in a mob by a Tory "wretch" brought out thousands of angry mourners. A few nights later a dispute over a barber's bill sparked a powder keg when a redcoat, tired of being taunted, struck a wigmaker's apprentice with his musket barrel.

CAST TO COMMEMORATE William Penn's charter, the Liberty Bell (above) gained fame by calling Philadelphians to hear the first public reading of the Declaration of Independence outside the State House. Shunning that building for its royalist ties, delegates to 1774's first Continental Congress met instead behind the fine Georgian facade of Carpenters' Hall (opposite).

A crowd formed instantly outside the King Street customhouse, opposite the State House. A corporal's guard, eight strong, pushed through, and the men loaded their muskets. Pressing in, a crowd pelted the redcoats with snowballs, rocks, and chunks of ice for about 15 minutes. Something heavy knocked Pvt. Hugh Montgomery backward on the ice. The soldier rose to his feet and fired into the crowd; the other redcoats followed suit.

Five dead included sailor Crispus Attucks, part Indian and part black, and Irish-born Patrick Carr. Six wounded men survived. Enraged Bostonians demanded vengeance. While the customhouse squad was jailed to await trial, the rest of the British garrison was removed from Boston. Copies of Paul Revere's inaccurate engraving of the Boston Massacre—as the event immediately became known—fanned fury throughout the colonies, where news of the revolutionary era's first blood stirred old discontents and framed new questions about British authority.

A cluster of paving stones in a traffic circle girdled by honking cars is all that marks the massacre site. Just beyond it the Old State House helps to frame the site in its 18th-century context. Dwarfed by office towers, these and other surviving revolutionary-era sites along Boston's three-mile Freedom Trail are powerful reminders of change unimaginable to 18th-century Bostonians who conceived of a new, independent nation. But these same sites also bear witness to the incredible changes that took place within the revolutionaries' own lifetimes.

Only a decade before the massacre, the street where it would occur was filled with cheering crowds as Massachusetts' royal governor announced King George III's accession from the Old State House balcony on Christmas Day 1760. A few months later, though, the State House served as a stage for the "first scene of the first act of opposition." In a four-hour speech, James Otis, lawyer for local merchants, argued against renewal of the crown's writs of assistance, general search warrants used by customs officials to look for smuggled goods.

"A Man is as secure in his Home," thundered Otis to a rapt audience, "as a Prince in his Castle." One of his listeners, the future President John Adams, wrote, "Then and there the child Independence was born."

Lieutenant Governor Thomas Hutchinson, an employee of the crown, was unmoved by Otis's eloquence, however. Four years later, the hated Massachusetts native got more than his comeuppance when a mob led by the Sons of Liberty ransacked Hutchinson's home as punishment for his rumored support of the Stamp Act. The mob "open'd his Beds and let all the Feathers out" and spent three hours slicing the cupola off his handsome brick mansion. The next morning Hutchinson appeared in the Old State House's council chambers with apologies for wearing the same clothes as the previous evening. "Indeed," he explained, "I had no other."

An Emblem of the Effects of the STAMP
O! the fatal Stamp

MELEE TURNS TO massacre, and in 1770 the patriot cause gains its first martyrs in front of Boston's State House. Paul Revere's engraving of the massacre (opposite), which shows a British captain urging his troops to fire, deliberately inflamed the settlers. Among pre-war indignities, none rankled more than the Stamp Act; a parody of the hated tax stamp appeared in the Pennsylvania Journal (above). Faneuil Hall, which served as Boston's "cradle of liberty," has been painstakingly restored (top).

THE STAMP ACT OF 1765, a direct tax on almost every scrap of printed paper, from tavern licenses to broadsides, spiked colonists' outrage as nothing before it had. In the Old State House, the Assembly installed a gallery so the public could watch the Stamp Act debate—and, as need arose, heckle and intimidate members who contemplated voting the Tory line. It was the first time in modern history that the public could observe their elected representatives at work.

Radically altered over the years, the State House's interior shows no trace of its public gallery, but the spacious meeting rooms of two other buildings still echo to the call of momentous events. Above the marketplace that "topmost merchant" Peter Faneuil built for Boston in 1742, Faneuil Hall was the secular pulpit of Sam Adams, "Man of the Town-Meeting." As a modern-day demagogue, Adams wouldn't have gotten far: He was dumpy, palsied, and so unkempt that his friends had to buy him decent clothes for public events. An abject failure at business, Adams excelled—brilliantly—at only one thing, political manipulation.

Exhorting and inspiring the Faneuil Hall throng, Adams created the Committee of Correspondence in 1772, a move soon copied by the other colonies. By the following year, crowds routinely overflowed Faneuil Hall's spacious pews as anger grew over a new tea tax. Meetings reconvened at Old South Meetinghouse, Boston's largest building. Even that meetinghouse couldn't contain the more than 5,000 people—nearly a third of Boston's population—who turned out on December 16, 1773, to hear demands that a cargo of the "bainfull weed" be returned to England.

As the meeting wore on, war whoops suddenly answered a signal from Adams, who was chairing the meeting. Faces smeared with lamp

Engrav'd Printed & Sold by Paul Revere Boston

black and red ocher, some 150 hatchet-wielding "Mohawks"—Adams's own Sons of Liberty—led thousands of onlookers to Griffin's Wharf by torchlight. Boarding three ships, the men smashed open chest after tea chest and heaved 60 tons of East India Company tea overboard.

Landfill long ago obliterated Griffin's Wharf, but the events there have galvanized Americans ever since. Other seaports held their own tea parties, but as the seedbed of resistance, Boston bore the brunt of Britain's swift punishment: the Coercive Acts. Better known to colonists as the Intolerable Acts, they closed the port of Boston, banned town meetings as "hotbeds of sedition," shifted political trials to England, and ordered troops to once again be quartered in Boston.

Faneuil Hall became a barracks—and then a theater for the troops' entertainment. In Old South Meetinghouse, Deacon Hubbard's beautiful carved pew was carried off to become a pig sty; the other pews were chopped into firewood, making way for the Queen's Light Dragoons' riding school and stables.

Rusticating at his Gloucestershire home, Gen. Thomas Gage was called back to America. In addition to commanding forces, he would become the governor of Massachusetts—the colony's own popular government was abolished. Breaking with precedent, Gage appointed royal judges—strong loyalists to a man. Many refused to sit, however,

RESOLUTE IN BRONZE, militia commander Capt. John Parker surveys Lexington Green. His small band of militiamen, assembled on the town common, confronted a column of 700 advancing British soldiers. Someone opened fire, and in the first battle of the Revolutionary War eight militiamen were killed.

fearing for their lives, and juries refused to serve. Paul Revere was a member of one of the first defiant juries. The brawny silversmith had long been known to Gage and his officers as a troublemaker. Revere's North End home, bought just a month before the Boston Massacre, became a martyrs' shrine a year later. During this "very striking Exhibition," thousands gathered in front of brightly lighted windows showing different scenes—here, the massacre; there, the ghost of young Christopher Snider; in the center, an allegorical Liberty grinding a British grenadier under her foot.

Already 90 years old when Revere bought it, his home in North Square is the oldest building in downtown Boston. The wooden house, spacious for its time, suggests the prosperity of an expert silversmith.

By 1775, however, Revere's customers in Boston's merchant class were feeling the pinch of the port closing; their misfortune became their artisans'. Idled except for his political activities, Revere began spending nights walking the streets with other unemployed craftsmen to keep watch over the British soldiers' movements and report back to patriot leader Dr. Joseph Warren.

Near midnight on April 15, all the ships' boats, previously hauled up, were rowed out to the men-of-war in Boston Harbor. Then, on the 18th, troops marched toward the bottom of Boston Common. A swirl of rumors in gossipy, spy-infested Boston indicated that Gage intended to seize the rebels' cache of arms in Concord and, possibly, arrest "principal actors" Sam Adams and John Hancock, who were holed up in the Lexington parsonage. Warren dispatched two riders to warn the men. Cordwainer William Dawes took the only overland route, sneaking through the town gate on Boston Neck with a squad of redcoats.

Revere's journey began with a meeting with his friend Robert Newman, sexton of Old North Church—then Boston's tallest building, today an active Episcopal congregation in the Italian North End. Newman's task, to hang two lanterns in Old North's steeple signaling Charlestown rebels of the British water route, was a delicate one. Redcoats swarming in the narrow streets might notice the lights, or a passerby might take them for a fire alarm. Revere himself had to row across the moonlit Charles River under the guns of H.M.S. *Somerset.* Safely in Charlestown, Revere borrowed a "very good Horse" from Deacon Larkin, who would never see it again. As Revere galloped through the night, a British patrol stopped him, seized his mount, and let him go.

By then, Revere, and several other messengers, had already passed through Lexington. There, men and boys waited through the long night, many huddling in Buckman Tavern, which still stands. Others who lived nearby went home to listen for a drumbeat calling them back to the green. Near dawn, it sounded. Revere, having walked back to Lexington, was close by: "The British Troops appeard on both Sides of the Meeting-House," he wrote. "In their Front was an Officer on Horse back. They made a Short Halt; when I saw, and heard, a Gun fired, which appeared to be a Pistol. Then I could distinguish two Guns, and then a Continual roar of Musquetry...."

No one knows who fired the first shot. British Maj. John Pitcairn tried to stop the infantry volleys that followed it, but to no avail. "The men were so wild they could hear no orders," wrote an officer. Weak, irregular fire from the few dozen Americans answered, and the skirmish was over in a minute or two. Eight militiamen died, ten were wounded, and one British private was grazed in the leg.

NORTH BRIDGE, *a replica of the original, spans the Concord, which reddened with the first British blood. Two minutemen also fell, but patriot hopes rose on the redcoats' disarray. Their retreat, noted Rev. William Emerson, was marked by "great fickleness and inconstancy of mind."*

Young Jonathan Harrington crawled to his doorstep, where he died at the feet of his wife and son, who had witnessed the shooting. Their white clapboard house still nestles by the tranquil green The fallen Americans were buried in a common grave on the green. Nearby, militia commander Capt. John Parker, in bronze, stands firm, his apocryphal words to his men etched in stone: "Stand your ground. Don't fire unless fired upon. But if they mean to have a war let it begin here."

On the morning of April 19, 1775, the smell of gunpowder still hung in the air when Captain Parker reassembled his determined little company, including several of the wounded. In ragged formation they marched to the Lexington town line, a distance of two miles, to face the British again. Throughout the countryside, the alarm had sounded. Farmers put down their plows, and parsons set aside their pens; grabbing their muskets, militiamen converged on Concord.

At Concord—the British goal all along—house-to-house searching yielded little, for the rebels had moved their cache. Grenadiers burned wooden carriages and utensils anyway. Seeing the flames, the 400 militiamen on Punkatasset Hill, half a mile away, feared the British were torching the town and advanced on three companies of regulars guarding North Bridge.

Panicky redcoats fired. Two Acton minutemen fell dead. American balls smashed into the poorly deployed British ranks, killing three men

"I KNOW NOT what course others may take, but as for me, give me liberty or give me death." With those words the fiery young member of Virginia's House of Burgesses gave a cause its battle cry in 1775. Thomas Sully painted him as statesman, but Henry played many roles. From tavern fiddler to business flop to Founding Father and four-time state governor, he symbolized a lasting American dream of hard-won success.

and wounding nine more. Both sides fell apart and scattered, ending the fight that was "physically so little, spiritually so significant."

The dead minutemen were taken to the home of Major Buttrick, which still overlooks the gentle slope of Punkatasset Hill. Fleeing redcoats left two of their own to be buried near the bridge, where the words of James Russell Lowell grace a slate table: "Unheard, beyond the ocean tide, Their English mother made her moan."

"The rude bridge that arched the flood," in the words of Concord resident Ralph Waldo Emerson, was removed in 1793. A replica of the original now spans the placid Concord River. More than monuments, though, history textures the whole landscape. Along the Battle Road, a National Historical Park, are houses and meadows, woods and stone walls where minutemen crouched and fired as the British fought their way back to Lexington. Reinforcements rescued them there; Munroe Tavern, east of town, became Brig. Gen. Earl Percy's headquarters. But, as provincials besieged them all along the route, the retreat to Boston turned into a bloody rout for the British, who suffered heavy casualties.

The next bloody clash came less than two months later. At Bunker Hill, overlooking Boston harbor, 1,054 soldiers, half the British force, were casualties—including Maj. John Pitcairn, whose son carried him dying from the battlefield. By the end of the hot June afternoon, the British had dislodged the Americans from their positions, now commemorated by a soaring obelisk. Bunker Hill, reflected British Gen. Henry Clinton, was "a dear bought victory, another such would have ruined us."

On May 10, 1775, cannons boomed at Fort Ticonderoga as the Second Continental Congress assembled in Philadelphia. Reconciliation with the mother country seemed a more remote possibility than it had the previous fall, when delegates to the First Congress had pledged allegiance to the Crown—and rejected "Acts of Parliament" that violated their rights as Englishmen. That first Congress had revealed sharp divisions among Americans in many ways. After arguing over a meeting place, for instance, the delegates rejected Pennsylvania's State House, with its royalist ties, in favor of Carpenters' Hall, now part of Independence National Historical Park. But a local Tory newspaper ominously warned that by offering their hall to Congress, the Carpenters risked having their necks "inconveniently lengthened."

Philadelphia, largest city in the colonies, was far less radical than Boston. From the beginning, William Penn's Quaker colony had welcomed all, and by the mid-1770s the City of Brotherly Love represented outlooks as diverse as its people's ethnic and religious backgrounds. In the narrow streets that Penn laid out, houses of worship from the era still open their doors. Betsy Ross and Benjamin Franklin occupied pews at Anglican Christ Church. Haym Salomon, a financier of the Revolution, lies in Mikveh Israel Synagogue's cemetery. George Washington honored France at St. Mary's Roman Catholic Church.

As pacifists, the Quakers opposed war. For Philadelphia's merchants and traders of all persuasions, prosperity blunted discontent. Fine Chippendale furniture and exquisite silver dazzled flinty New Englanders when they visited grand houses such as Samuel Powel's, which still stands on Third Street. So did the Philadelphians' sophisticated lifestyle. The well-to-do read books from Benjamin Franklin's Library Company, America's first subscription library—then housed in Carpenter's Hall, now in Library Hall. They relaxed at Schuykill River fishing clubs, some still in existence, and at public houses like City Tavern—a restaurant today—which John Adams called the "most genteel" in the colonies.

For average Philadelphians, however, British rule increasingly chafed. Taxation was so complex and so onerous that it even determined the physical details of tradesmen's dwellings that survive in places like Elfreth's Alley, the nation's oldest residential street. Only a prosperous tradesperson could afford a home bricked in the heavily taxed Flemish bond pattern, or a dwelling more than two bays wide. Dwellings built with only a few small windows suggested their owners' tight budgets, as homes were taxed not only on the number of panes but also on their size.

JOHN ADAMS
1735-1826

"THE REVOLUTION was in the minds and hearts of the people," wrote the man who would become the new nation's second President. As one who witnessed—and helped guide—"this radical change" from Boston's earliest unrest to the Treaty of Peace in 1783, Adams, more than anyone else, would define that change for future Americans in his vast, insightful writings.

AMONG ITS LESS AFFLUENT CITIZENS, Philadelphia counted a newly arrived English immigrant named Thomas Paine. He had failed in every line of work he tried, from corset making to tax collecting, but Paine was an inspired essayist and pamphleteer. In January 1776 he published "Common Sense," a slender pamphlet containing a powerful argument for independence. Paine explained that Americans' belief that the British Constitution protected them was an illusion. Moreover, the constitution itself was founded on the evils of monarchy and aristocracy: Far from having honorable origins, monarchies were established by "the principal ruffian of some restless gang, whose savage manners…obtained him the title of chief among plunderers…." To the argument that Britain was the parent country, Paine answered, "Even brutes do not devour their young…."

"Common Sense" kindled the fervor for independence as nothing else had. Within months 100,000 copies had been printed and read throughout the colonies. The Second Continental Congress in Philadelphia had been moving, John Adams said, like a "Coach and six—the swiftest Horses must be slackened and the slowest quickened." Though they had created an army and a navy, authorized privateers, opened negotiations with France—and even met openly in the State House—the delegates had also petitioned the king for reconciliation. "Common Sense" brought a sea change, and the Congress moved with it.

In the Assembly Room on June 7, Virginian Richard Henry moved "That these United Colonies are, and of right ought to be, free and independent States, that they are absolved from all allegiance to the British Crown, and that all political connection between them and the State of Great Britain is, and ought to be, totally dissolved." With the middle colonies "not yet ripe," Congress put off a final decision until July 1, and 33-year-old Thomas Jefferson was given the task of drafting a declaration of independence.

At his desk in the second-floor rooms he rented from a German-born bricklayer, Jefferson labored for two weeks. Alterations and omissions—notably Jefferson's diatribe against slavery—were made by other delegates. Almost half a century later, *(continued on page 86)* 81

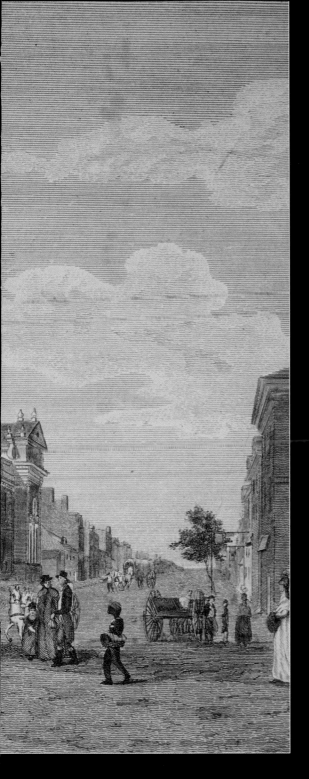

N O LONGER **William Penn's "greene Countrie Towne," Philadelphia by the late 18th century boasted the greatest gathering of wealth, industry, commerce, culture, and people in America. In a tinted engraving by William Birch, buildings stretch along Second Street to the horizon (left). The congregants of white-steepled Christ Church symbolized a city of class divisions and political tolerance; affluent, they included loyalists and patriots throughout the war. Under the roof of the market, next door, a cornucopia of goods bespoke the city's enviable location between fertile soils to the west and bounteous waters to the east. Congressional delegate John Adams wrote that he feasted "upon a thousand delicacies" each day. In one engraving Philadelphians share oysters from a street cart (above).**

INDEPENDENCE HALL

MOMENTOUS EVENTS occurred in Philadelphia's Independence Hall (above). Around the candlelit tables of the Assembly Room (above, right), the Second Continental Congress named George Washington commander in chief of the Continental Army in 1775 and adopted the Declaration of Independence the next year. There the Founding Fathers approved an official American flag in 1777, ...ed for the

Articles of Confederation in 1781, and drafted the Constitution in 1787. Brief wartime use as British quarters left "the inside torn much to pieces," as one delegate lamented. When Philadelphia undertook a restoration for the Centennial, the Assembly Room contained paintings and cast-off furniture; among the few remaining original pieces glinted the silver inkstand used to sign both the Declaration and the Const...tion (opposite).

STERLING SILVER INKSTAND
INDEPENDENCE HALL

*STARS AND STRIPES flies
again over Fort Stanwix
in upper New York State,
as legend says it did
for the first time in any
battle in 1777. With
the British advancing on
Philadelphia, Americans
won an important
moral victory at this
Northern Campaigns
site, beating back a siege
force of redcoats, Tories,
Hessians, and Indians.*

Jefferson wrote that he had aimed not at "originality of principle or sentiment," but rather at "an expression of the American mind." As such, the document solemnized on July 4, 1776, had exerted its amazing power far beyond American shores during Jefferson's own lifetime.

Broadsides of the Declaration of Independence were printed. At noon on July 8, Col. John Nixon of the Pennsylvania militia read a copy to a huge crowd in the State House yard—now Independence Square. Bells, including the Liberty Bell, rang all day. Toward evening, the king's coat of arms was torn off the courtroom wall and "burned amidst the acclamations of a crowd of spectators." Philadelphia was now the new nation's capital.

In New York City, Gen. George Washington, commander in chief of Continental forces, had the Declaration of Independence read at the head of every brigade. Soldiers roared approval, and then joined jubilant townspeople spilling down Broadway toward the Battery. At Bowling Green, Sons of Freedom toppled the gilded equestrian statue of George III. Its two tons of lead, according to one newspaper, were "to be run into bullets, to assimilate with the brains of our infatuated adversaries, who, to gain a pepper-corn, have lost an empire."

THAT CONCLUSION WAS PREMATURE. Though the British had evacuated Boston three months earlier, by early July they were massing their greatest expeditionary force ever around Staten Island under the command of Adm. Lord Richard Howe—whose brother William commanded British Army troops. Aided by hired Hessians, the British pushed the Americans off Long Island, and then sued for peace. Redcoats ferried a Congressional delegation, including the elderly Benjamin Franklin, from Perth Amboy to Staten Island's Billopp House, which still stands.

Peace terms politely rejected, both sides shouldered their weapons again. On Manhattan Island the Americans fought erratically. At Kip's Bay they melted in the face of cannon fire from ships in the East River. An exasperated Washington struck fleeing officers and lamented, "Good God, have I got such troops as those!" A day later, however, the Americans drove the British from the woods and fields of Harlem Heights.

Hopelessly outgunned, the patriots gave up Manhattan—but not until fire gutted the British prize. Suspecting arson, the British exacted revenge by summarily executing the American spy Nathan Hale on Long Island. On the gallows, Hale declared, "I only regret that I have but one life to lose for my country."

Hale's words contrasted starkly with the disorder and demoralization of American forces as they fell back to White Plains, then across New Jersey and into Pennsylvania late that fall. Whole brigades contracted "cannon fever" and skulked home. Gen. Henry Knox declared the army "a receptacle for ragamuffins." Washington recognized the effect that poor pay, brief enlistments, misery, and fatigue had on his forces. He begged Congress for clothing and appealed to New Jersey and Pennsylvania for troops, which were not forthcoming. Without the "speedy enlistment of a new army," he wrote, "I think the game will be pretty well up." Thomas Paine, with Washington for the humiliating retreat, wrote of "the times that try men's souls."

General Cornwallis pursued the tattered army to the banks of the Delaware River. Washington's men, however, had removed or destroyed every boat on the New Jersey side, preventing the British from following them into Pennsylvania. Then, warfare being a seasonal activity for European armies, the British snugged down until spring in their winter quarters, leaving an outpost of Hessians to guard Trenton, ten miles from the river. Urged by his aides, Washington agreed that "dire necessity, will, nay must, justify an attempt" on Trenton.

In present-day Bucks County, Washington Crossing Historic Park preserves the scene of that 11th-hour gamble. In the Thompson-Neely House, on a ridgetop above the icy river, Washington and his officers plotted the Christmas strike, while men suffering from "swamp fever" languished down the hall. On Christmas the men held their usual evening parade under the bare oaks and hickories. Instead of returning to their huts, they marched to the river, some barefoot and bleeding, others with rags tied around their feet. Wind-driven snow and hail lashed them, "but I have not heard a man complain," wrote an aide.

At 3 a.m., that aide sat writing in McConkey's Ferry Inn. The plan was hours behind schedule as Marblehead fishermen tried to pilot unwieldy Durham boats laden with men, horses, and cannon through fast-moving ice floes. Yet Washington, wrapped in his cloak, seemed never "so determined as he is now." Flintlocks iced over and supporting divisions didn't arrive, but the delay barely mattered. In Trenton, Commandant Col. Johann Rall, who called the Americans "country clowns," was sleeping off his Christmas cheer while his Hessians fell apart. A thousand returned to Pennsylvania as American prisoners.

Not content to savor victory, Washington left his campfires burning by the Delaware and stole a night march to Princeton, where savage

fighting bested the British in less than an hour. At winter quarters in Morristown smallpox struck, but the British remained inactive until the end of spring.

While Gen. Henry Clinton held New York and Gen. John Burgoyne, in Canada, prepared a southward thrust, Gen. William Howe and 15,000 men sailed up Chesapeake Bay. Washington was fortified by several thousand new Continentals, pledged to fight through the war, and by one important volunteer, the 19-year-old Marquis de Lafayette—wounded when Americans saw defeat at Brandywine. Marching onward, the British entered Philadelphia on September 26, 1777; Congress had already fled to Lancaster, and the city seemed half deserted.

The main British army encamped at Germantown, six miles northwest. There, buildings that witnessed the Revolution still crowd approach routes the Americans used to attack the British on a foggy

"PARADE WITH US, my brave fellows, there is but a handful of the enemy, and we will have them directly." Washington's words to his exhausted, half-naked army at the Battle of Princeton inspired some of the war's most savage combat, and a hard-won victory just days after the one at Trenton. Officers rally their troops in an oil painting by William Mercer (left). Wintering in Morristown, Washington awaited fresh recruits— and his first French volunteers, including the 19-year-old Marquis de Lafayette. Joseph Boze later painted the decorated marquis in dress uniform (above).

October morning. As Gen. John Sullivan's column drove redcoats down the road, British fire erupted from inside Cliveden, the gracious stone home of Benjamin Chew, Pennsylvania's Chief Justice.

Every year, the reenactment of the Battle of Germantown recalls defeat snatched from victory's jaws. Company after company of Americans attempted to storm the mansion. Musket fire from second story windows picked off some of the patriots, and Cliveden's heavy wooden doors proved invulnerable to battering rams. "The most horrid fog" mingled with a blinding pall of gun smoke. So great was the confusion on Cliveden's verdant lawn that Americans who had marched all night and not eaten in 24 hours accidentally fired at each other.

Though the Americans suffered 700 casualties, Washington said the "day was unfortunate rather than injurious." The troops were in better form than ever, and a few days later word came of Burgoyne's

BATTLE OF GERMANTOWN

GUN SMOKE *screens Cliveden, home of Pennsylvania's Chief Justice, Benjamin Chew, in an early depiction of the Battle of Germantown (below, bottom). Each year British turn an American victory into an 11th-hour rout during a reenactment of the battle (below).*

In reality, several factors led to Washington's defeat at Germantown. His plan, which called for four approach routes, proved too complex. Demanding surrender from 120 British holdouts in Chew's house was fatal. After occupants killed the officer bringing the summons, enraged Americans attacked Cliveden with field pieces and musket fire. Cannonballs tore the doors off their hinges, but the British rehung and barricaded them, frustrating the Americans' storming. Dense fog and smoke added to the confusion.

Nearly a year later, Chew called his Georgian home "an absolute wreck." Restoration returned it to its former grandeur (opposite). Many of Chew's fine furnishings and artworks had escaped destruction. Today, they grace the interior of the mansion (below).

"*SAT. 18TH TO FRI. 31ST: Continuing…building our huts…very cold & almost Starved for Want of Provision….*" A soldier's diary limns the winter of despair at Valley Forge, Pennsylvania. A 19th-century engraving captures the grim dejection of the troops (above); they knew the well-fed British army reveled in nearby Philadelphia. Washington spent Christmas Day planning a surprise move against the city—but then thought better of it. In the wake of defeats at Brandywine and Germantown, critics began to question his competence. Drifted cannons (right) recall the trying winter at Valley Forge, now a national park.

surrender at Saratoga on the Hudson River. That decisive victory proved the war's turning point, as France took notice of its opportunity to join the winning side against its old nemesis. On February 6, 1778, American delegates signed a treaty of alliance in France. That same day, though, Washington, at Valley Forge, described his men as "starving."

Some 18 miles west of Philadelphia, the winter camp was actually a windblown ridge that rose away from the Schuykill River. The site offered natural defenses and was well located to guard the colonies' interior against British forays. But there was little in the way of supplies. Farmers in the area discovered that the British paid more for provisions—and that they paid in solid English coin. Until the energetic Gen. Nathanael Greene became quartermaster in late winter, the army's provisioning system was in total disarray. Men went for days without food, or ate only firecake for weeks. Albigence Waldo, a surgeon, recalled "a bowl of beef soup, full of burnt leaves and dirt, sickish enough to make a Hector spew."

Little remains—but the words of men who suffered through it—to convey that winter's ordeal. Though the weather was not severe, poor sanitation spread disease that felled men already weakened by hunger.

Stout, red-faced Frederick Steuben arrived in late February 1778 bearing a bogus Prussian title and a much-embellished war record. But his military abilities were real. From dawn until dusk he drilled men on the thawing, muddy parade field, teaching the discipline and crisp maneuvers of a professional army. By early May the army could showcase its transformation at a grand celebration when "the Good News" of the French alliance finally arrived.

London had already reacted to the "News." While Britain manned its Caribbean islands against French attack, it instructed General Clinton, Howe's successor, to evacuate Philadelphia and mass forces in New York. Not all of the troops marched north, however: Thousands of the men turned to unleash attacks on southern cities, hoping to awaken a sleeping giant of Tory sentiment there.

For a while it seemed as though the plan might succeed. The southern states were thinly defended. Washington was in New York bottling up the British and trying unsuccessfully to plan joint efforts with the French. Elsewhere, a scattered war effort saw John Paul Jones's *Bonhomme Richard* and a fleet of privateers harassing British shipping, while on the frontier, young Col. George Rogers Clark hunted the British and their Indian allies. By New Year's Day 1779, the British pocketed Georgia, though it took them more than another year to pound Charleston into submission in one of the Revolution's most devastating defeats. That disaster, lamented a South Carolina congressman, left Americans with nothing but "a few discontented, fluctuating militia" in the south.

At Camden, South Carolina, troops under Cornwallis crushed the Americans. But the "fluctuating militia" began to come into its own. Patriot bands waged guerrilla war, and Gen. Nathanael Greene's battered army of only 1,500 men settled for harassment while it rebuilt strength. At King's Mountain, "overmountain men" and their long rifles vanquished 1,100 Tories. At Cowpens, Virginian Dan Morgan, Greene's superb second in command, placed his men in widely spaced lines and exhorted his sharpshooters to "Pick off the epaulets!" The renowned brutality of British Col. Banastre Tarleton made his defeat that much sweeter. Then Morgan pressed on to reunite his forces with Greene's at Guilford Courthouse, where, on March 15, 1781, Cornwallis paid dearly for a victory. Cowpens, Kings Mountain, and Guilford Courthouse are today all national battlefields.

UNABLE TO WIN THE CAROLINAS, Cornwallis's tired army pulled back to Virginia. The state fell easily: Governor Thomas Jefferson, despite warnings from Washington, hadn't girded for an invasion, and he himself was nearly taken prisoner when Tarleton's cavalry galloped into Charlottesville. Only Lafayette's three regiments continued to bedevil Cornwallis, the Englishman boasting in vain that "the boy cannot escape me," as the Frenchman dogged him to the mouth of the Chesapeake. The British wanted to establish an anchorage to guard their seaboard supply lines between New York and Charleston, and Cornwallis set about fortifying Yorktown.

Clinton, in New York, disapproved of the Virginia invasion and refused Cornwallis's request for reinforcements. Instead, he ordered Cornwallis to send 3,000 troops to New York, where, he correctly feared, a Franco-American invasion was in the works. In August everything changed when Washington received news from Adm. François de Grasse that his French Caribbean fleet was sailing to Chesapeake Bay and would stay there until mid-October.

Washington did not hesitate: He and the Count de Rochambeau secretly spirited their troops out of New York and marched them 450 miles south to risk all on a victory at Yorktown. At the end of September, the last detachments joined Lafayette's men and de Grasse's sailors. The French fleet had already sealed off Yorktown and fired their guns until the British fleet "crowded on sail and turned away."

The Revolutionary War came to a close on the bluffs of an arrow-shaped peninsula overlooking the York River, now preserved as part of

Colonial National Historical Park. Cornwallis's elaborate fortifications—including 10 redoubts, 19 batteries, and 65 guns—crumbled as French and American gunners pounded them. While bombshells streaked across the sky like meteors, men dug parallels and zigzags in sandy ground, burrowing ever closer to the enemy. On the night of October 14, American and French troops dodged grenades to take British redoubts numbers nine and ten—both now rebuilt for tourists.

Mounting the enemy parapet on the morning of October 17, a redcoated drummer beat a parley while an officer waved a white handkerchief. Cornwallis requested that two officers from each side meet "at Mr. Moore's house, to settle terms for the surrender of the posts of York and Gloucester." At the farmhouse—restored after a Civil War gutting—negotiations dragged into the early morning of the 19th. Around noon Washington received the articles of surrender in the captured redoubt number ten, and, after signing, added a line: "Done in the trenches before Yorktown, in Virginia, October 19, 1781."

The afternoon of the formal surrender was warm. The French were trim and crisp in white broadcloth and shining black gaiters. Across from them the Americans stood in hunting shirts and tattered uniforms, men who had endured six terrible years for this moment. Finally came the redcoats to ground arms, playing "The World Turned Upside Down." As John Bull's fife and drum fell silent across the land, Americans responded in their own ballad of Yorktown:

His music soon forgets to play
His feet can no more move, sir,

And all his bands now curse the day
They jigged to our shore, sir."

The work of nationhood was just beginning. At the war's outset only a desire for liberty united Americans. During the 1780s they realized they shared a vision of representative government—but remained divided on its specifics. As history revisited Independence Hall in 1787, delegates to the Constitutional Convention created a framework—"a republic, madam, if you can keep it," quipped an aged Franklin—and a Constitution that would become models for democracies everywhere.

TATESMAN

THOMAS JEFFERSON

STATESMAN · INVENTOR · DIPLOMAT · PRESIDENT
1 7 4 3 - 1 8 2 6

"IT IS A PART of the American character to consider nothing as desperate; to surmount every difficulty by resolution and contrivance," wrote Thomas Jefferson, then American minister to France, to his 14-year-old daughter Patsy.

By the 1780s Jefferson could use the Revolution itself as proof, on a grand scale, of that statement's truth. If, on the personal level, he sounded like an unbending parent, he led by example: Perhaps no historical figure has better personified American "resolution and contrivance." Both qualities seem evident in a portrait of him by Rembrandt Peale (above).

Jefferson was born to the privileges of Virginia's first families, but his multitudinous accomplishments were uniquely his own. By the age of 30 he read seven languages; he acquired a profound understanding of mathematics, engineering, paleontology, zoology, botany, and archaeology.

He was an innovator and a noted architect, an agronomist and a musician. As statesman, Jefferson combined active roles—President, governor, minister—with philosophical ones. He attacked established churches, primogeniture, and slavery, though to the bafflement of succeeding generations, he kept his own slaves. He planned a public education system and a less brutal criminal code. In the space of six weeks, he drafted both Virginia's Statute for Religious Freedom and the Declaration of Independence.

Jefferson's tomb records both these documents as two of his proudest accomplishments. The third was his founding of the University of Virginia in Charlottesville. He designed the school's classically proportioned buildings (opposite) in his old age.

Service in France whetted Jefferson's inspiration for architectural elegance. He admired little else about transatlantic "luxury and dissipation," favoring instead a republic of yeoman farmers and, for himself, a life of rural simplicity at his beloved home, Monticello, outside Charlottesville, Virginia.

MONTICELLO

HOME OF THOMAS JEFFERSON

FOUR DECADES of "putting up and pulling down" finally left Jefferson with the home he wanted—Monticello (above). Service to his country repeatedly lured him from his mountaintop home; not until his homecoming from France in 1789 did the dome begin to take shape.

The furnishings within Monticello bespeak a singular mind. So that he might never be far from his work, Jefferson's bed occupied an alcove linking study to sitting room (opposite).

Of hundreds of innovations he promoted, Jefferson regarded the polygraph as the "finest invention of the present age."

THE POLYGRAPH
MADE A COPY OF A DOCUMENT
AS IT WAS PENNED.

WAGONS AND HORSEMEN *surge toward a setting sun in an idealized western landscape entitled "The Oregon Trail"*

CHAPTER 4

WESTWARD EXPANSION

BY SCOTT THYBONY

by Albert Bierstadt. Tepees in the background symbolize the Native American presence in this 1869 oil painting.

E ARLY IN THE LAST CENTURY stories of the American West began filtering back to towns and settlements. The tales told of vast plains spreading beneath continental skies, of mountain peaks so high the snows never melted. With those narratives, a westward longing took hold.

Intrigued by the region beyond the Mississippi River, President Thomas Jefferson sent an expedition up the Missouri in 1804. Although he never ventured west of the Appalachian Mountains himself, Jefferson instructed Meriwether Lewis and William Clark to explore the vast Louisiana country, recently acquired from France.

The first transcontinental expedition of the United States left St. Louis and crossed the Great Plains by riverboat. After winding through the Rockies on horseback, the explorers followed the Columbia River to the Pacific Ocean. They entered an uncharted region so immense it took months of hard traveling to comprehend its scale. From the start, the explorers established good relations with most of the Native Americans they encountered. The success of the expedition depended on the Indians' willingness to provide geographic information and horses for crossing the mountains.

After Lewis and Clark returned in 1806, fur trappers followed in their wake. They pushed to the headwaters of the Missouri River and beyond, coming to know the twist and tumble of every stream from the Spanish Peaks to the Mountains of the Wind. As the mountain men explored the farthest reaches, settlers poured into the new territory along the Mississippi. By 1820 almost 30 percent of the American population had settled west of the Appalachians.

Emigrants began traveling overland to Oregon and California in the 1840s. The trappers, who had spent years on the margins of society, found themselves in the vanguard of a great migration. They now put their hard-earned knowledge to use guiding emigrants across the mountains to the Pacific Coast. The first of these overlanders were farmers, drawn by the prospects of free land. Mormons soon followed, searching for religious freedom; other adventurers sought gold. Some emigrants were merely curious or caught up in the wave of excitement; some were escaping the past, bent on making a new life for themselves.

In this wide sweep of historic events, the human scale often gets lost. A sense of detachment takes its place, making it difficult to recognize ourselves in the people who lived those times. But all it takes to reconnect with the past is reading a few lines from the diary of a pioneer woman caring for her child or the account a young scholar traveling with a free-ranging band of Lakota Sioux. And sometimes all it takes is wandering into a living-history encampment.

Wood smoke drifted through the trees above a party of fur trappers camped on the Laramie River in eastern Wyoming. The pungent

PIONEER WOMEN, honored by a bronze statue in Ponca City, Oklahoma (above), endured great privations as they crossed unbroken plains and mountains as rugged as those rising above the western desert of Utah (opposite). Families traveling west faced incredible obstacles and often relied upon sheer force of will to make a new life in the West.

smoke mingled with the aroma of cooking meat in an old layering of scents. One mountain man, a skinning knife sheathed at his back, watched a rack of buffalo ribs roasting over the coals. Others lounged about, repairing gear and talking.

Suddenly a rider galloped up, shouting a warning. He had seen dust rising in the distance, marking the approach of an unknown horseman. "OK, boys," said the captain, Rex Norman, "grab your guns and look friendly."

ON MOST DAYS, Rex wears the gray and green uniform of a park ranger. Today, the chief interpreter at Fort Laramie National Historic Site had donned his buckskins to stage a fur-trapper encampment with a dozen hand-picked reenactors.

A Lakota Sioux dressed in fringed leggings with an eagle feather dangling from his beaver-fur hat rode into camp. He made signs indicating his desire to trade, each gesture precise and expressive. A skilled sign talker can convey far more than the gist of a simple message. Mountain man Jim Bridger once entertained a gathering of Lakota for more than an hour using sign language. The circle of onlookers gasped at the appropriate moments and laughed at the punch lines, hanging on each gesture as the grizzled mountaineer related his story without uttering a single word.

Dismounting, the Lakota filled a pipe with tobacco, and one of the trappers spread a blanket on the ground. Joined by a couple of his companions, he sat cross-legged as the pipe was passed around the

SETTLERS CROWDED into the region between the Appalachian Mountains and the Mississippi River after the War of 1812. A log cabin marks the site of the farm in southern Indiana (above) where Abraham Lincoln spent his pioneer boyhood. Trails, such as the Natchez Trace (opposite), drew homesteaders to the banks of the Mississippi and set the stage for the next wave of western migration.

107

LEWIS AND CLARK

EXPLORERS, NATURALISTS, CARTOGRAPHERS, & ADVENTURERS

I N 1804 President Thomas Jefferson sent Meriwether Lewis (above, right) beyond the Mississippi River to learn about the vast and little-known region recently purchased by the U.S. from France. Choosing William Clark (above, left) to share the responsibilities of leadership, Lewis organized a 43-man expedition called the Corps of Discovery.

Jefferson instructed Lewis to collect precise information on the region they traversed and to search for a route to the Pacific Ocean, hoping the Corps could locate the rumored Northwest Passage. Lewis was to study the customs of the tribes encountered and establish good relations as a basis for future trade. With an eye toward settlement, the President asked for a detailed report on the region's plants, animals, and minerals. Jefferson arranged for the leading scientists of the day to train Lewis.

Lewis and Clark left the frontier settlement of St. Louis in the spring of 1804 and traveled up the Missouri River by keelboat and dugout canoe. After wintering near Mandan Indian villages on the Missouri, they continued their journey across the plains. Failing to find a water route, they crossed the Rocky Mountains on horseback and followed the Columbia River to the Pacific. The Corps of Discov-

ery spent its second winter at the mouth of the Columbia. Almost two centuries later, waves lap the Oregon coast at Ecola Point (right), near the expedition's winter quarters.

Lewis and Clark carefully recorded their observations and shipped back specimens. They filled their journals with sketches of such items of interest as the "Pheasant of the Rockies," a fish from the Columbia, and an illustration of how one tribe practiced flattening foreheads.

The explorers returned to St. Louis in 1806, successfully completing their mission and providing a wealth of reliable information. The nation's first transcontinental expedition revealed the geography of an immense and diverse territory, inspiring an era of exploration and stirring the imagination of a nation turning westward.

circle. After they completed the ritual smoke, the men began dickering, using only hand signs. Rex Norman watched the bartering from the sidelines. "For some reenactors," he said, "it's a form of recreation. But here it's re-creation. We are trying to re-create the past."

REX ONCE TRAVELED to the site of the first mountain-man rendezvous, part of the way on horseback. "I felt a glimmering of it in those mountains," he said. "Sometimes when the wind hits you just right, you look over your shoulder and all of a sudden realize that what you're seeing, hearing, smelling is the same thing they felt in 1825. No different. My brother-in-law felt it at the same time—just a glimmer, but it was there."

Certain places make room for the past. Fort Laramie, a partially restored frontier outpost in eastern Wyoming, is one of them. "Few places in America," Rex Norman said, "influenced history over so long a period. Fort Laramie was born of the frontier, and it made that frontier possible. When civilization passed it by, the fort became redundant. The last soldiers left in 1890, the same year a congressman unofficially declared the end of the frontier."

The story of the American West played out against the backdrop of Fort Laramie. A young trapper, arriving at the fort in the 1830s, could have witnessed the entire cavalcade pass by during the span of a single lifetime. He could have heard a cavalry bugler sounding "Boots

and Saddles," a fiddler playing "Oh! Susanna," or drumbeats coming from an Indian camp. He might have heard the crack of a whip as Calamity Jane drove a freight wagon to the goldfields, or the creak of handcarts pulled by Mormons on their way to the Great Salt Lake.

Remnants of the old army post of Fort Laramie cover the earlier fur-trapper fort, but beyond the parade grounds enough of the historical landscape remains to set the scene—high plains, a line of distant mountains, and a sense of time rolling back to 1834. In that year trappers built the first of a series of forts near the confluence of the Laramie River and the North Platte. From this location on the edge of the plains, trails reached north and south along the mountain front, east to the Missouri River and west across the Rockies to the Columbia. From this geographic crossroads, a fur company could draw the buffalo trade of the prairies and control supply routes into the mountains.

The army purchased the outpost that would become Fort Laramie in 1849 to protect the growing influx of emigrants. Wagon trains rolled along the Platte River route as settlers, gold seekers, and Mormon converts trekked overland in a vast, westward-reaching migration. Some emigrants took the Santa Fe Trail through the Southwest, but most chose the northern routes. Trails leading to Oregon and California began at today's Independence, Missouri, and crossed the plains to the south bank of the North Platte River. The Mormon Trail began at Council Bluffs, Iowa, and traced the river's north bank until

INDIANS AND TRADERS MINGLE *inside Fort Laramie in a scene painted by Alfred Jacob Miller in 1837. Established*

where the plains meet the Rockies, the trading post became a major supply station for western-bound emigrants.

Jim Bridger
1804-1881

Heading west in 1822 to trap beaver, Bridger began acquiring a detailed, firsthand knowledge of the Rocky Mountain region. He put this experience to good use in later years as a trader, army scout, and guide. The famous frontiersman eventually returned east, ending his long career on a Missouri farm.

Fort Laramie. All of the trails followed the same route to South Pass, the main wagon crossing of the Rockies at the southern end of the Wind River Range in present-day Wyoming. Once beyond the pass, the emigrant routes branched off toward their separate destinations. Eventually half a million overlanders traveled up the North Platte, as a nation—no longer confined between the waters of the Atlantic and the Mississippi—began to dream of a continental destiny.

In 1977 Geoff Barnard and his friend Newell Searle spent 45 days hiking the Oregon Trail. They covered more than 600 miles between Scotts Bluff, Nebraska, and Soda Springs, Idaho. Change had come so slowly to the country they walked through that they could recognize it from the descriptions left by the earlier travelers. On their journey they passed only a few people as they crossed miles of wide-open ranch lands.

"We experienced a sense of remoteness," Geoff said, "the absence of a visible human presence. My most enduring impression of the Oregon Trail is that there's more solitude now than then."

Wheel ruts still mark portions of the Oregon Trail, but pinpointing those marks of hard travel can be difficult. Field historian Bob Rosenberg has studied Wyoming trails for more than a dozen years. "When you read the diaries and look at the maps, it's all so clear," he said, "but once you're out there, it's so vast that everything gets lost."

The most visible section of the Oregon Trail crosses Deep Rut Hill west of Fort Laramie, where travelers had to climb bluffs to avoid the river. Wagon traffic, both emigrant and military, funneled over the rocky spur before fanning out on the far side. Countless wagons had worn ruts into the bottom of a trough cut five feet into solid bedrock. In the fine dust at the bottom of the ruts, a set of deer tracks indicated the old trail was still getting some use.

Back at the living-history encampment, sunlight glimmered on the Laramie River as Kirby Werner stepped into the current. The water darkened his buckskin pants below the knee, the wet fringe hanging heavy. The mountain man drove a long stake into the streambed as a pair of greenhorns watched, listening carefully to his instructions on how to set a beaver trap.

A REMARKABLY SIMILAR SCENE was sketched by Alfred Jacob Miller, the only artist to paint the mountain man from life. In 1837 Miller joined an expedition led by Capt. William Drummond Stewart, a former British officer with a passion for the American West. Captain Stewart had encouraged the young artist to accompany him to the annual fur-trade rendezvous on the upper Green River. He wanted a visual record of his overland adventures and the unsurpassed scenery of the Rocky Mountains to hang in his Scottish castle.

They reached Fort Laramie after more than a month on the trail. While at the fort, Miller sketched dramatic views of it. The stockade walls rise above a treeless plain with the Laramie Mountains, a spur of the Rockies, in the distance. The Stars and Stripes flies boldly above the fort, and blue streamers hang from the tips of tepees pitched on a plain alive with feathered horsemen.

Inside the walls the artist found the hollow square crowded with Indians from throughout the northern plains and Rockies. They mixed with traders from as far away as the desert Southwest and Pacific Northwest, free trappers and company men, and "Kentuckians, Missourians, and Down Easters." It was a time of long-distance traveling in a region where the best trails consisted of no more than a pair of wheel ruts. In a view of the interior Miller painted, Plains Indians wrapped in colorful blankets and buffalo robes cluster around warming fires. A pack mule stands loaded and waiting, and, on the parapet wall above it, something catches the interest of a man peering through a spyglass.

Stewart's party continued to the Wind River Range, known to them as the Mountains of the Wind. When the expedition reached its destination on a tributary of the Green River, Miller encountered his first rendezvous. This tumultuous affair, combining a trade fair and annual blow-out, drew together several hundred mountain men and about 3,000 Indians. Miller sketched the swirling scene, documenting the brief historical convergence when descendants of Europeans lived in cultural parity with Native Americans. In a series of panoramic views, Miller rediscovers the lost wilderness of an earlier America transplanted to the Mountain West.

What Alfred Jacob Miller found, however, was already ending. As the artist worked, he was unaware this was the last great rendezvous. Miller was the only artist to record the classic period of the Rocky Mountain trapper, roughly 1820 to 1840. He arrived after the fur trade had peaked, and the way of life it made possible would soon disappear, but his work helped create an image, still with us, of the wild, free West.

That sense of freedom surfaces in his notes. During a violent storm at night, he relates, a trapper was "sitting cross-legged in Indian fashion, with his hands over the expiring ashes. His features pinched with cold, and lank and thin, wore a comically serious expression as the electric flashes lighted them up;—the rain streaming from his nose & prominent chin, & his hunting shirt hanging about him in a flabby & soaking embrace;—spite of such a situation which was anything but cheering, he was rapping out at the top of his voice a ditty, the chorus or refrain of which was, & which he gave with peculiar emphasis:

How happy am I!
From care I'm free:
Oh, why are not all
Contented like me?"

Captain Stewart, a veteran of the Battle of Waterloo, enjoyed the companionship of these free trappers. He completed his first trip to the Rockies in 1833 and returned each summer, determined to experience the life of the hunter while it lasted. In a novel based on his western travels, Stewart conveys the emotion of entering a country still unsettled, unknown. *(continued on page 122)*

SAMUEL CLEMENS
1835-1910

SAMUEL LANGHORNE Clemens, after piloting a Mississippi riverboat, traveled west in 1861 to the mining camps of Nevada. He published a lively account of his overland stagecoach journey in Roughing It. *Writing under the pen name Mark Twain, Clemens became one of America's finest authors and humorists.*

THE OREGON TRAIL

B EGINNING IN THE EARLY 1840s, the first wave of western migration sought Oregon as its destination. Canvas-topped wagons (below) served as mobile homes for families who spent four to five months on the trail. For many, reaching new homes in the Northwest required crossing 2,000 miles of rugged—sometimes waterless—terrain.

The Oregon Trail followed the south bank of the Platte River, skirting Scotts Bluff (left), a rocky outcrop in western Nebraska that served as a landmark.

Other trails later tunneled through the natural corridor the Platte River Valley offered. Wheels gouged tracks into the bedrock of Deep Rut Hill in Wyoming (right), a visible reminder of the estimated 500,000 emigrants who headed west in the greatest migration in United States history.

THE CALIFORNIA TRAIL

C ALIFORNIA-BOUND TRAVELERS branched off the Oregon Trail after crossing the Rockies at South Pass. Routes veered south, linking scarce water and grass with passes over the Sierra Nevada. A streambed snakes across an alkali flat in the Fortymile Desert of present-day Nevada, one of the most dreaded sections of the California Trail. Reporter William A. Wallace recorded his impressions during a traverse of the route in 1858. "This forty miles," he wrote, "is the terror of the whole route, and no wonder. These bleaching bones and rusty irons are evidences the sight of which makes one wish to hurry on, and not feel safe until they no longer greet the eye. I never saw a desert before, and I do not wish to see another."

THE SANTA FE TRAIL

FOLLOWING AN INDIAN trade route once used by Spanish explorers, Capt. William Becknell blazed the trail that would become a vital artery linking the U.S. with territory acquired from Mexico. Becknell and four companions left Missouri on a trading expedition in the fall of 1821. Mexico had gained independence from Spain, and, hoping the new republic would permit them to trade with its northern province, the men turned south toward Santa Fe. "A continual and almost uninterrupted scene of prairie meets the view as we advance…," Becknell recorded in his diary.

When Becknell's party reached the old pueblo at Santa Fe, the Mexicans welcomed the traders—and their loaded packhorses. Becknell sold his goods at enormous profit and returned the next year. Other traders quickly followed, and soon freight wagons were rumbling across the wide prairie.

Crumbling adobe walls remain of Fort Union, established on the edge of the central plains in 1851 (top). To protect travelers, the army built this outpost and major supply depot near the junction of two main branches of the Santa Fe Trail.

Traces of the route, where freighters cracked their whips and soldiers marched in columns on their way to the Rio Grande, still slice across the prairie (opposite). Bypassed by the railroad in 1879, Fort Union became obsolete; the military abandoned it in 1891. Chimneys now stand guard facing the old parade grounds along officers row (above).

121

EMIGRANTS STARTING late or delayed on the trail faced the threat of deadly winter storms (right). In 1856 the Mormon Church began organizing handcart companies. Unable to afford ox-drawn wagons, but determined to reach Salt Lake City, Mormon converts pulled two-wheeled carts overland from Iowa City, about 235 miles east of the Missouri River, following the Mormon Trail. The last two companies, totaling 1,076 pioneers, began the long trek late in the season. Caught by blizzards on the Sweetwater River in present-day Wyoming, some 200 handcarters died in the snow and cold. An emigrant who preceded them left his name on Register Cliff, west of Fort Laramie (above).

"An indefinite, but not insensible awe," he writes, "creeps over one whose uncertain way lies through these dreary wastes; and although the ever-present dangers of these regions, may confine his thoughts to the immediate objects around, there is yet a strong impulse felt to wander still farther, and to plunge still deeper into the unknown wilds of these Western woods."

IN 1843 STEWART MADE a final trip to the Rockies before returning to Scotland. That same year, explorer John C. Frémont passed through Fort Laramie on his way to the Great Salt Lake. After making a winter crossing of the Sierra, he returned by a southern route to complete an epic circuit of the Far West. His maps and reports encouraged the Mormons to settle in the Great Basin a few years later and guided miners to the California goldfields.

Beginning in 1853, military expeditions searched for a practicable route to build a transcontinental railroad. In the course of their work, they often undertook scientific investigations. The desire to gather geological knowledge drew explorer John Wesley Powell down the uncharted Colorado River in 1869. He became a national hero when his expedition descended the Grand Canyon for the first time. Two years later he returned with a survey team to map the surrounding region.

Some people went west to make discoveries; others to leave the past behind and push beyond the constraints of memory and tradition. A young Harvard graduate, who would become one of America's greatest historians, headed west to find the past.

Francis Parkman reached Fort Laramie in 1846, at a pivotal moment in the opening of the West. The United States had annexed Texas, leading to war with Mexico, and would soon take California and New Mexico. That year the government settled the boundary dispute with Britain over Oregon, opening a vast territory to settlement. Parkman saw the West during a period of aggressive expansion—when the nation doubled in size and overland migration began in earnest. But the young scholar had little interest in the events churning around him.

Making a conscious attempt to re-create the past, Parkman left Boston for a chance to live among nomadic tribes in their "primitive state." Only 22 years old, he had already chosen his lifework—to write the history of the great struggle between France and England for North America. To do that job right, he needed to understand the character of the Native Americans.

Francis Parkman sat in the main gateway of Fort Laramie, below the painted figure of a red horse stretched out in a run. Adobe walls had replaced the earlier wooden stockade. As a trader finished telling

him a story, a band of Lakota Sioux appeared on the opposite bank of the Laramie River. Wild and chaotic, the procession began to cross. Parkman had traveled for weeks by steamboat and horseback for moments like this.

"Men and boys, naked and dashing eagerly through the water," he writes in his journal, "horses with lodge poles dragging through [with] squaws and children, and sometimes a litter of puppies—gaily attired squaws, leading the horses of their lords—dogs with their burdens attached swimming among the horses and mules—dogs barking, horses breaking loose, children laughing and shouting…."

LESS THAN A CENTURY BEFORE, the Oglala, the largest of seven western Lakota bands, crossed the Missouri on their own western migration. They drove out every tribe they encountered, taking the Black Hills from the Kiowa and Cheyenne in about 1800. Drawn south by the new trading post, they arrived on the Laramie River in 1834. When a band left for the hunting grounds on the Laramie plains, Parkman decided to follow it. "I am now a scholar in a rougher school," he wrote his mother.

The young historian, dressed in fringed buckskins and a red flannel shirt, tracked the Indians over the mountains. After days of wandering, he found the village encamped in a great circle of lodges on the upper reaches of the Laramie River. The Oglala had come to procure buffalo hides and lodge poles to replace their worn tepees. A high basin stretched beyond, "a vast green uniformity, forlorn and tenantless…." The plains around Laramie were contested; Shoshone, Arapaho, and other tribes claimed the region.

After several days of cautious traveling, the Oglala scouts reported finding a buffalo herd within striking distance. As the women pitched the lodges, the men rode off in "a wild, helter-skelter, hurrying group." Wearing only a loincloth and moccasins, each hunter carried a bow in one hand and a quiver slung over the shoulder. The men turned toward the Medicine Bow River.

"Riding upward in a body," Parkman later wrote, "we gained the ridge of the hill, and for the first time came in sight of the buffalo on the plain beyond….

"We were among them in an instant. Amid the trampling and the yells I could see their dark figures running hither and thither through clouds of dust, and the horsemen darting in pursuit. While we were charging on one side, our companions attacked the bewildered and panic-stricken herd on the other. The uproar and confusion lasted but a moment. The dust cleared away, and the buffalo could be seen scattering…while behind them followed the Indians riding at furious speed, and yelling as they launched arrow after arrow into their sides."

When the chase ended, Parkman found Big Crow, an Oglala headman, butchering a buffalo. His son was by his side, eating the raw liver. Lakota hunters believed it gave them strength and courage. Parkman, the gentleman from Boston, accepted a piece and found it excellent.

After nearly three weeks with the buffalo nomads, Parkman came back to Fort Laramie disillusioned. A dose of firsthand experience had blunted the edge of his romanticism. Returning to the East, he worked his notebooks into the American classic *The Oregon Trail*. His

GRANITE CLIFFS overlook the cold waters of Donner Lake, high in California's Sierra Nevada (opposite). Trapped by winter storms just short of the pass in 1846, a party of 91 emigrants led by George Donner remained snowbound for five months. They built crude huts and cabins near the frozen lake—and waited for spring. Starvation led to madness and cannibalism in a grim ordeal that cost the lives of almost half the stranded party.

MINERS RUSHED to California after the discovery of gold nuggets (below) at Sutter's Mill in 1848. As new finds occurred, fortune seekers raced from one goldfield to the next. Some boomtowns survived; others disappeared. The Swazey Hotel survives snow in the ghost town of Bodie, founded as a California mining camp in 1859 (opposite). An 1876 lithograph illustrates subsurface operations at Gold Hill in Nevada's Comstock (left).

sense of realism and his portrayal of Native Americans as distinct individuals, both unusual for the time, created a dramatic travel narrative. Like Alfred Jacob Miller's paintings of the fur trappers, Parkman's book remains a vivid record of a way of life that soon vanished.

On the Oregon Trail that summer of 1846, all was in motion, all in flux. Less than a hundred people had made the crossing five years earlier, and now nearly 3,000 overlanders were passing Fort Laramie. The rising tide of emigration would peak in 1852, when 52,000 took the trail, many of them bound for the goldfields of California.

These new emigrants differed in one essential respect from the earlier explorers and fur traders. Many traveled as families, intent on finding a new home. When he first arrived at Fort Laramie, Parkman had watched the post trader steady his spyglass and focus on a string of white-topped wagons in the distance. "The families are coming," the trader shouted. Women now added their voices to the story of the West, and the diaries and letters they left still reach across the years.

"In the first place," Louisa Cook wrote her sister, "this is one of the greatest old trips that was ever heard of…think of not sleeping in a bed for 6 or 7 months…wandering for weeks among the mountains— teams nearly worn out—provisions nearly gone…you would laugh to see us come into camp about 3 every afternoon tired hungry & of course cross—ragged shoes, every article of clothing trimmed with fringe (all the style here), hoopless, spiritless & disposed, would we give way to our feelings, to be disatisfied with every thing—but after supper what a change—some 6 or 8 camp fires burn brightly round the corell & round these a cheerful group of men & women seated on a

JOHN C. FRÉMONT, in a wildly exaggerated engraving, plants the American flag on what he thought was the highest summit in the Rocky Mountains. Although he chose the wrong peak, the man who would come to be known as Pathfinder managed to explore much of the West in a series of well-publicized expeditions. His maps and reports helped open the region to settlement.

box, inverted pail, or true Indian style squatted on the ground laughing over the exploits of the day & cracking jokes at one anothers expense—truly, with all that is disagreeable there is much that is enticing about this wild gipsy life."

Some women, traveling by wagon for months, gave birth on the trail. Men buried the mothers and babies who died en route. Together men and women found strength in moments of despair.

"It's morning," Keturah Belknap wrote in her diary. "I have been awake all night watching with the little boy. He seems a little better; has dropped off to sleep. The sun is just rising and it shows a lot of the dirtiest humanity every was seen since the Creation. We just stop for an hour and eat a bite and let the teams breath again. We divide the water with the oxen. George has sat on his seat on the front of the wagon all night and I have held the little boy on my lap on a pillow and tended him as best I could. I thot in the night we would have to leave him here and I thot if we did I would be likely to stay with him but as the daylight, we seemed to get fresh courage."

Not everyone found the strength to go on. Some turned back, and some were buried beneath the trail itself. The emigrants faced danger, suffering about one death for every twenty pioneers who lived. They feared Indians, but died from disease, accident, and sometimes starvation. The Donner Party, trapped in the snows of the High Sierra and reduced to cannibalism, lost 42 of its 91 members. But it was not the worst tragedy.

Brigham Young, the dynamic head of the Mormon Church, began leading his followers west in 1846. Fleeing persecution for their religious beliefs, especially the practice of polygamy, they trekked to the Great Basin and founded Salt Lake City. For many years converts from the United States and Europe continued to follow the Mormon Trail to their Utah sanctuary.

In 1856 the Mormon Church began organizing converts into handcart companies. Two-wheeled handcarts, cobbled together at little expense, could be pulled and pushed by hand. For those unable to afford the luxury of a wagon and team, these vehicles provided the only chance to reach Salt Lake. The first three companies completed the journey successfully, but endured great hardships.

"3d August. Sunday." So wrote Twiss Bermingham, a graduate of Dublin University and a member of the second handcart company. He had undertaken the trek with his wife, Kate, and three children. "Started at 5 o'clock without any breakfast and had to pull the carts through 6 miles of heavy sand. Some places the wheels were up to the boxes and I was so weak from thirst and hunger and being exhausted with the pain of the boils that I was obliged to lie down several times, and many others had to do the same. Some fell down. I was very much grieved today, so much so that I thought my heart would burst— sick—and poor Kate—at the same time—crawling on her hands and knees, and the children crying with hunger and fatigue. I was obliged to take the children and put them on the hand cart and urge them along the road in order to make them keep up. About 12 o'clock a thunder storm came on, and the rain fell in torrents. In our tent we were standing up to our knees in water and every stitch we had was the same as if we were dragged through the river. Rain continued until 8 o'clock the following morning."

Bermingham's company took 15 weeks to pull their handcarts some 1,400 miles, and on their arrival at Salt Lake City, they danced in the streets. The last two companies that year were not so fortunate. Both groups got a late start on the trail after their ships were delayed sailing from England. An early winter caught them far from their destination. Cold weather, hunger, and overexertion took a tremendous toll. Of the 1,076 handcarters who began the journey, many suffered frostbite and more than 200 died.

"Our old and infirm people began to droop," writes John Chislett, "and they no sooner lost spirit and courage than death's stamp could be traced upon their features. Life went out as smoothly as a lamp ceases to burn when the oil is gone." Stranded by deep snow, many of the emigrants died before a rescue party from Salt Lake City arrived.

"Shouts of joy rent the air," Chislett writes of their deliverance, "strong men wept till tears ran freely down their furrowed and sun-burnt cheeks, and little children partook of the joy which some of them hardly understood, and fairly danced around with gladness. Restraint was set aside in the general rejoicing, and as the brethren entered our camp the sisters fell upon them and deluged them with kisses." The handcart brigades continued until 1860, when the last company reached Utah without a single fatality.

WHEN JOHN WESLEY Powell made the first descent of the Colorado River in 1869, the one-armed Civil War veteran became a national hero. His account of the expedition, written years later, includes a story of his res cue from a cliff high above the Green River. An old engraving depicts the drama as boatman George Bradley pulls Powell to safety.

A S THE MORMONS SETTLED the Great Basin country, word of a gold discovery at Sutter's Mill in California reached the eastern settlements. Gold fever quickly swept the nation. In 1849, 30,000 people headed for the diggings by land, and nearly that many journeyed by sea. During the next several decades, miners chased a series of gold rushes from Pike's Peak in Colorado to Silver City in Nevada and the Black Hills of South Dakota.

Soon a stage line carried passengers on the California Trail, and an express mail service began operating in the spring of 1860. Riding relays, horsemen for the Pony Express could cover the 2,000-mile distance in only ten days.

"'HERE HE COMES!'" Mark Twain recounts the approach of a mail rider in his book *Roughing It*. Twain was in a stagecoach east of Fort Laramie, on his way to the mining camps of Nevada. "Away across the endless dead level of the prairie a black speck appears against the sky, and it is plain that it moves. Well, I should think so. In a second or two

RUST RED PINNACLES of Canyonlands National Park, in Utah, recall the country Major Powell revisited in 1871.

He repeated much of his earlier river journey and undertook the systematic mapping of the area.

TREELESS PRAIRIES forced settlers to improvise when building their homes. To conserve lumber, they dug their cabins into hillsides. Nebraska pioneer Sylvester Rawding and his family posed outside their sod house for an itinerant photographer in 1886 (opposite). A South Dakota storm approaches the Prairie Homestead, built in 1909 (above). Snug inside thick walls of sod during the blizzard of 1873, one homesteader listened to the wind outside. "Made one's ears hum and buzz all the time," she recalled.

it becomes a horse and rider, rising and falling, rising and falling—sweeping toward us nearer and nearer—growing more and more distinct, more and more sharply defined—nearer and still nearer, and the flutter of the hoofs comes faintly to the ear—another instant a whoop and a hurrah from our upper deck, a wave of the rider's hand, but no reply, and man and horse burst past our excited faces, and go winging away like a belated fragment of a storm!"

WITH THE COMPLETION OF THE TRANSCONTINENTAL telegraph line in the fall of 1861, the Pony Express became obsolete. It ceased operations shortly after Twain's trailside encounter. Even during the Civil War, however, westward migration continued, with 15,000 settlers staking claims under the Homestead Act of 1862. A farmer could acquire title to 160 acres of federal land without purchase after making improvements on it for five years. Work on a railroad linking coast to coast also began during the war. Crews laid track east from Sacramento and west from Omaha. They met at Promontory, Utah Territory, in 1869, to complete the first transcontinental railroad.

Under pressure from settlers and speculators, the federal government opened unoccupied lands in Indian Territory to settlement. In 1889 the government announced the opening of a large tract in central Oklahoma. At high noon on April 22 gunshots started the first of the most famous land rushes in the history of the U.S. Nearly 100,000 hopefuls on horseback and in wagons raced to claim a farm or town lot. Within a single day they had staked out every available site.

As mining towns sprang up almost overnight and cattlemen moved onto the buffalo plains, Native Americans throughout the West

found themselves confined to reservations. In our image of the frontier, this meeting of cowboy and Indian leads to a tragic resolution, sudden and violent. At times it did, but descendants of the ranchers who stayed often tell a story with a different ending. Robert and Michele Cross live on the Tomahawk Ranch, on the north end of the Laramie Mountains near the junction of the Oregon and Fort Fetterman Trails. In 1875 Robert's grandfather, George Cross, arrived in Wyoming behind a herd of cattle. "He always wore a suit," Robert said, "even when on horseback."

Robert recounted a story his grandfather told him about those final years of the frontier. George Cross once got caught in a raging blizzard when he was returning from Laramie Peak. Snow drifted 20 feet deep in the creek bottoms and trapped him for five days. Those came close to being his last days. Cattle, blinded by the storm, wandered into the ravines and floundered. "In spring when it finally melted," Robert said, "they found cows in the tops of trees where they got stranded in the drifts."

Above the Cross ranch house, on a ridge where the buffalo grass grows, stone tepee rings mark an old encampment. Plains Indians were still hunting buffalo in this valley when George Cross and his cattle first arrived.

"My granddad liked Indians," Robert said. "He never had any trouble with them—but once." Riding alone across the high plains of Wyoming, George glanced over his shoulder and spotted an Indian horseman on his trail. Worried, he tried to lose him—but couldn't. His pursuer kept gaining on him. When the Indian finally caught up to George Cross, he took one look at the cowboy.

"'Wrong man,' was all the lone horseman said. Then he rode on."

133

PROMONTORY,
UTAH TERRITORY

I N 1862 CONGRESS authorized the building of a transcontinental railroad. The federal government subsidized the undertaking with funds and land grants. Work on the 1,776 miles of track began in earnest after the Civil War. The Central Pacific Railroad pushed east from California while the Union Pacific raced westward across the Great Plains. The railroads brought problems as well as people. Buffalo scatter before an oncoming train in a period engraving (above); Indians, aware of the new threat to their means of subsistence, attacked railroad work crews. On May 10, 1869, the tracks met at Promontory. The last spike was driven, linking the Atlantic and Pacific coasts by rail (opposite) and effectively ending the way of life of the Plains Indians.

HORSES STUMBLED and wagons overturned on September 12, 1893, as more than 100,000 hopefuls raced to stake

their claims in Oklahoma's Cherokee Outlet; gunshots at high noon signaled the start of the last great land rush

CHAPTER 5
STRUGGLE & STRIFE

BY SCOTT THYBONY

WAVES OF UNION SOLDIERS charge Confederate defenders on Marye's Heights during the Battle of Fredericksburg.

Union officer Frederick Cavada painted his compatriots struggling to maintain order during the futile assault.

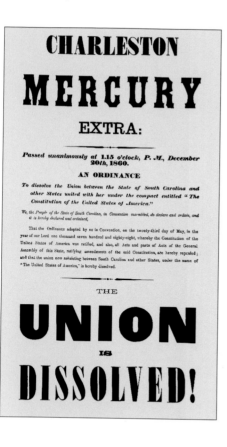

HEADLINES SCREAM the end of the Union after South Carolina voted to secede on December 20, 1860. The North insisted the United States could not be split, but the Civil War did just that — dividing states, towns, and families during the four-year struggle. Mist settles over the Vicksburg battlefield, where a monument honors the Wisconsin infantrymen who died in Mississippi (opposite).

BIRDS EXPLODED FROM THE TREES, startled by the roar of cannon fire. As the acrid scent of black powder drifted over the rolling fields of Virginia, more than 2,000 Civil War re-enactors gathered to re-create the First Battle of Manassas. Confederate regiments were forming on the crest of a hill as columns of Federal soldiers marched into the swale below. With bands playing and flags flying, they spread out in a battle line. "Right oblique," shouted an officer on horseback. "Forward!"

His orders echoed the aggressive spirit of a time when America struggled to reshape itself. For half a century, roughly from the fall of the Alamo in 1836 to the surrender of the Apache warrior Geronimo in 1886, the nation grew rapidly. It was a time of national strife, when the central government grew in power, asserting control over Indian tribes and breakaway states. It was a time of lost causes and last stands, from the Alamo to Appomattox and from the Trail of Tears to the Little Bighorn.

In the West warfare flared along the frontier wherever American Indians resisted encroachment on their lands. To the south, the Texans won their independence, leading to war with Mexico when the United States annexed the new republic. Battles raged from California to the Mexican capital in a dress rehearsal for the greatest struggle of that tumultuous period. As the Civil War opened, soldiers who had attended West Point together found themselves commanding opposing forces. Friends suddenly faced each other as enemies in a tragic struggle that would fundamentally change the character of the nation.

A sense of collective loss echoes through the history of the Civil War. The four years of warfare came as a tremendous shock, and the first battle, fought at Manassas in 1861, hit the hardest. This first major engagement typified in many ways the entire conflict. Military tactics, inspired by Napoleon, had not caught up with the advances in modern weapons and resulted in horrendous casualties. Romantic illusions of warfare quickly crumbled, but the idealism of both sides survived the loss. The great sacrifices of that first battle drew such a sharp line between opposing visions of America that no compromise was possible. The war had to be fought until one side achieved a clear victory.

To commemorate the battle that the South would call Manassas and the North, Bull Run, reenactors had traveled thousands of miles to Leesburg, Virginia. "The emotions you experience are real," said Sam Frankl, who had come from California to march with the Tiger Rifles. The night before, Sam and his comrades had slept in the rain, rolled only in blankets. They bivouacked without tents for the sake of authenticity and now appeared authentically haggard. "Sometimes there's a moment, just a passing moment," Sam said, "when the give-and-take is just right and you have a glimmer of what it must have been like."

As the rolling fire of muskets passed down the line of bluecoats and sputtered to an end, a soldier dropped slowly to the ground with hands outstretched to break his fall. "Some of them are just terrible at dying,"

THE OLD SOUTH

Echoes of the antebellum South linger at Oak Alley, a Louisiana mansion framed by ancient live oaks (left). A wealthy planter built the estate along the Mississippi River during the 1830s.

"The air was fragrant with these trees and shrubs, as well as from old fashioned roses," said Emma Falconer, of her childhood near the Mississippi. "There was the cinamon, the York and the Demascus together with the beautiful Cherokee rose which trailed over the garden wall and was crowded with the jasmine and the honeysuckle."

Plantations, and the life of ease and refinement they supported, depended on slavery, but most southern farmers worked small holdings without slaves. Since cotton had to be picked by hand, plantations became increasingly dependent on slaves to meet the growing demand from northern mills. Sharecroppers continued the practice of handpicking cotton after the Civil War (below). Southerners shipped cotton to distant markets from gracious coastal cities such as Charleston, South Carolina, shown in a view of the East Battery painted in 1831 by S. Barnard (below, left).

STEAM ROLLS SKYWARD as stevedores load a paddle wheeler at a New Orleans river landing in a painting by Hippolite Sebron. The southern states depended on rivers and seaports to export their agricultural products and import manufactured goods. Without an industrial base of its own, the Confederacy was vulnerable to a coastal blockade by the North.

Betsy Daly remarked. The Pennsylvanian, dressed in period clothes, watched the action from a distance. She had created an impression of a Union officer's wife by wearing a hoopskirted silk dress and stayed in character as she told me, "I shouldn't even be talking to you without the proper introduction."

Bodies littered the field by the end of the staged battle, although some of the dead watched the closing moments with their heads propped up. Behind them flashed the red lights of an ambulance coming to remove a victim, not of an enemy bullet, but of the heat.

As the guns fell silent, Charles R. Norris III of Leesburg entered the cemetery grounds next to the re-enactment site. He had not attended the day's events. Under a great, overarching tree he found the grave of his namesake, Cdt. Charles R. Norris. Splotches of yellow-green moss edged a headstone bearing the inscription, "Killed In Battle At Manassas Junction VA. July 21, 1861. Aged 17 Yrs 2 Mos. & 9 Dys." So young, they counted each day.

B Y A TWIST OF FATE, the cadet from Virginia Military Institute was leading soldiers into battle on the day he died. Norris had stayed in school at the outbreak of war, too young to enlist, until ordered to escort a shipment of gunpowder to the Confederate Army. Col. Thomas J. Jackson, desperately in need of drillmasters, kept the young cadet to train his recruits. Given the rank of acting captain on the eve of battle, 17-year-old Norris followed Jackson to Manassas.

The cadet's great-great nephew stood by his grave 135 years later and recounted the story of the battle he had heard growing up. "They were in the trees," said Norris, speaking with a soft Virginia accent, "when the orders came to charge. He jumped up and shouted, 'Quick boys, and we can whip 'em!' At that moment he was hit in the chest by a bullet or shrapnel; we're not sure which. That was the end of it for him."

Rumblings of war could be heard two years before the armies met at Manassas. On a fall morning in 1859, a restless crowd watched as a contingent of United States Marines moved into position on the grounds of the federal armory in Harpers Ferry. They had arrived under the command of Col. Robert E. Lee to suppress an insurrection. Two thousand spectators filled the narrow streets of the town, wedged between the Shenandoah and Potomac Rivers in the Blue Ridge Mountains. They had come to witness the end of a violent standoff with a band of northern abolitionists intent on freeing slaves. Fear of an uprising was sweeping through the southern states, but events were moving toward a different kind of war, one they did not fear enough.

Inside the brick enginehouse, John Brown, the man who dreamed of leading a slave revolt, waited for the attack. One of his sons lay dead at his feet, and another was dying. A handful of abolitionists stood with Brown, but not a single slave had willingly joined his "army of liberation." The northern raiders held 11 hostages and had already taken the lives of 3 townsmen. The first person they shot and mortally wounded was the railroad baggage man, ironically a black man.

Gray hair bristling, John Brown held a cocked rifle as Lt. J. E. B. Stuart walked up to the heavy oak doors and handed him a message from Lee demanding his unconditional surrender. When the abolitionist hesitated, wanting to bargain, Stuart jumped aside with a wave of his hat. At that signal, the storming party charged the enginehouse to the cheers of the crowd.

At Lee's orders, the dozen marines carried unloaded guns to reduce the risk of injuring the hostages. They battered in the door and rushed inside with fixed bayonets. Two attackers fell in the gunfire, but the others pressed on. They quickly overwhelmed the defenders and captured those who remained alive. All hostages were rescued unharmed, bringing the 36-hour uprising to an end.

Failure had haunted the life of John Brown; the raid at Harpers Ferry was only his last defeat. Wounded in the attack, he had to be carried into the courtroom for his trial. A jury soon found him guilty of murder, treason, and inciting a slave revolt; the presiding judge sentenced him to death by hanging. Supporters offered to help him escape, but he refused, knowing his death would force the nation to face the corrosive issue of slavery. By sacrificing himself in a just cause, John Brown would turn his final failure into a moral victory.

On December 2, the day of his execution, the abolitionist handed a prophetic note to one of his guards. "I John Brown am now quite <u>certain</u> that the crimes of this <u>guilty</u>, <u>land: will</u> never be purged <u>away</u>; but with Blood. I had <u>as I now think</u>: vainly flattered myself that without <u>very much</u> bloodshed; it might be done."

A horse-drawn wagon carried the prisoner, seated on his own coffin, to the gallows. Guarded by 1,500 militiamen, Brown climbed the steps to the hangman's noose without faltering. Among the troops was a company of cadets from Virginia Military Institute. With them stood Thomas J.

WORKERS POUR MOLTEN iron for cannons at the West Point Foundry in New York State; the painting by John Ferguson Weir reflects gloomy factory walls. Rich farmlands and fisheries linked with booming manufacturing centers gave the northern economy a clear advantage on the eve of the Civil War.

JOHN BROWN
1800-1859

JOHN BROWN, embittered by the border wars in Kansas, took the fight against slavery to the South. In 1859 he attacked the federal armory at Harpers Ferry with what former slave Frederick Douglass termed "the force of a moral earthquake." Soon captured by United States Marines, the abolitionist stood trial for murder, inciting a slave revolt, and treason. In a 1942 painting by Horace Pippin, Brown rides to the gallows seated on his own coffin (right).

Jackson, an undistinguished professor but resolute soldier, who admired the condemned man's "unflinching firmness."

With the election of Abraham Lincoln a year later, South Carolina voted to secede from the Union, and other states soon followed. Cheering crowds gathered in towns throughout the South, spurred on by fiery speeches and martial music. On April 12, 1861, Confederate forces began bombarding Union-occupied Fort Sumter in Charleston Harbor—a clear act of war. Soon after the firing on the flag of the United States, Lincoln called for 75,000 volunteers to end the rebellion. Filled with patriotic zeal, recruits streamed into hastily organized camps as both sides mobilized for war. One hundred days after the opening shots, two American armies would clash in the first major battle of the Civil War. Before the war's end hundreds of thousands of soldiers would die in the bloodiest conflict in American history. Their sacrifice would fulfill John Brown's prophecy and redefine the nation.

By the start of the Civil War, differences between regions had grown acute. Manufacturing towns in the North were growing in importance, while agriculture still dominated the South. New York and Pennsylvania each manufactured twice as many goods as all the southern states combined. Vast, slaveholding plantations came to characterize the South, but most farmers continued to work small holdings. Since northern factory workers accounted for 90 percent of the country's industrial output, the region felt confident of a quick victory. The agricultural South depended on slavery and cotton exports vulnerable to blockade. Many southerners, however, believed their military traditions and fighting spirit would carry them through what most believed would be a short conflict. The *New York Times* predicted the rebellion would end within 30 days.

The South believed it had the right to leave the Union and defend its borders against invasion. It fought for the right to choose its own destiny. The North disagreed. It saw the American people as one nation and fought to preserve the Union. Slavery was the emotive force underlying the conflict, but only later in the war did abolishing it become a declared goal of the North.

The day after Virginia seceded, Federal soldiers set fire to the arsenal and abandoned Harpers Ferry. Col. Thomas Jackson, in his first command as a Confederate officer, seized the armory and held the strategic town while volunteer forces gathered. Skirmishes and minor engagements built toward a massive, violent confrontation.

"Dear Mother," wrote Charles Norris from Harpers Ferry, where he had just turned 17. "Not being dead yet I thought I would attempt to write another letter and give you a little news....We have about fifteen thousand troops here and it is the prettiest sight in the world to see them drilling. They cover all the fields and hills."

As the Confederate forces at Harpers Ferry grew in strength, Gen. Joseph E. Johnston assumed overall command, with Jackson serving as a brigade commander. A Federal Army was concentrating its forces across the Potomac River. Their orders were to keep Johnston's troops from joining the main Confederate Army at Manassas Junction, 30 miles southwest of Washington, D.C.

On July 18, with J. E. B. Stuart's cavalry screening its movements, Johnston's army slipped away and marched swiftly to the nearest

railhead. Acting captain Charles Norris boarded a train for Manassas with the rest of Jackson's brigade. Expecting a sharp fight for the vital rail junction, the young officer was about to enter his first battle. "We will give Old Abe's troops a pretty hard shake," he wrote home.

The main Union Army under Brig. Gen. Irvin McDowell had left Washington a couple of days earlier. Pressured into action, he had ordered his 35,000 troops to cross the Potomac and engage the Confederates. Spirits ran high. Many soldiers looked forward to closing with the enemy. As bands played "John Brown's Body," the largest army ever assembled in North America lumbered toward Manassas.

McDowell reached the crossroads of Centreville on July 18. He faced a Confederate Army of 22,000 under Brig. Gen. Pierre G. T. Beauregard, deployed behind the steep banks of Bull Run. The Union general sent a force to probe a ford on the road to Manassas, but it stumbled into a hot engagement and fell back. McDowell, who had never led men in battle, hesitated. For two days the general waited as reinforcements from the valley swelled the Confederate ranks.

The long roll sounded early on the morning of July 21, waking the soldiers of the Second New Hampshire Infantry. Carrying cartridge boxes filled with ammunition, they joined a column of Federal soldiers moving up Bull Run under the cover of darkness. McDowell was attempting an end run around the Confederate defenses. At first light he hoped to take the enemy by surprise and sweep down its exposed line. Even with inexperienced officers maneuvering green troops over unfamiliar terrain, his plan almost worked.

"We were in the woods," wrote Ai B. Thompson, a lieutenant with the New Hampshire regiment, "when the firing began and the balls whistled thro' the trees past our heads in double quick....The men threw away their blankets, rushed thro' the woods into the open field in the direction of the enemies' fire."

Three hours behind schedule, the Union Army launched its attack. The Confederates, even slower in comprehending the danger, rushed reinforcements to check the Federal advance. But resistance collapsed as regiment after regiment forded Bull Run and crowded onto the battlefield. Outflanked and overwhelmed, the Confederates fell back in disorder.

"Victory! Victory!" cried General McDowell as he galloped behind the lines. "The day is ours." So far it was, but at the moment his enemy gave way, McDowell hesitated. His careful plans had unraveled. He paused to shuffle his troops, trying to reform regiments before the final push. Distracted by details, the Union general lost sight of the overall battle, and his army stalled at the foot of Henry Hill.

"We...drew up in line awaiting orders," Thompson wrote, "all the while cannon balls and shells flying and bursting about our ears.... Our men began to grow unsteady under the enemy's fire, our commanding officers didn't seem to know what to do."

JUDITH HENRY, BEDRIDDEN FOR YEARS, listened in terror to the shriek and thud of artillery as the battle swirled around her farmhouse. The 85-year-old widow had lived most of her life on the broad, undulating hilltop, now surrounded by fallow fields. The commanding elevation that gave her a fine view of distant mountains also drew the warring armies toward her home.

Newly promoted General Jackson, with his eye for terrain, found a strong defensive position on Henry Hill. He formed his brigade a few hundred yards from Mrs. Henry's house, sheltered from direct fire and screened by a thicket. J. E. B. Stuart's cavalry guarded his flank. Cadet Norris and the other Virginia soldiers hugged the ground as shells burst overhead and trees splintered around them. Remnants of regiments fled past, and the wounded hobbled to the rear, soaked in blood. "Steady, men," said the general as he calmly rode along the line, "all's well."

Galloping toward his retreating troops, Gen. Barnard Bee reined in his horse and pointed his sword toward the Virginians. "Look, men, there is Jackson standing like a stone wall!" he shouted, and a legendary nickname emerged in the heat of battle. "Let us determine to die here, and we will conquer! Follow me!"

Early in the afternoon, McDowell ordered two batteries forward. The Federal artillery unlimbered on the hill within a few hundred yards of "Stonewall" Jackson's cannons. The position was in advance of their own troops—exposed to enemy fire, and vulnerable to attack. Recognizing the danger, Capts. J. B. Ricketts and Charles Griffin reluctantly deployed their batteries on each side of the Henry house. As they readied their cannons, Union gunners began to receive enemy fire from the direction of the farmhouse. A blast of shots from Ricketts's guns silenced the sharpshooters, but a shell exploding inside ended the life of Mrs. Henry.

A few miles east sightseers had crowded onto an open ridge near Centreville to watch the battle. Journalists and army officers mingled with Washington's finest who had ridden out for the occasion. Hoopskirted ladies escorted by men in frock coats followed the action by the booming of distant guns and puffs of bluish *(continued on page 154)*

ISSUES DECIDED ALLEGIANCE
WEST POINT GRADUATES

UNION GENERALS

ULYSSES S. GRANT

WILLIAM TECUMSEH SHERMAN

GEORGE B. McCLELLAN

CONFEDERATE GENERALS

ROBERT E. LEE

THOMAS J. "STONEWALL" JACKSON

J. E. B. STUART

WAR DIVIDED the nation, forcing former West Point classmates to make a difficult choice. Almost all the graduates from the South chose to serve with their native states; they owed their allegiance, they felt, to home and family rather than the nation. Officers who had fought side by side in the Mexican War now faced each other as enemies.

Prominent Confederate and Union generals graduated from the military academy in New York. West Point cadets, subject to strict discipline and given a rigorous education in engineering and science, became civilian as well as military leaders for the nation. Mementos of war, cannons (above) overlook the Hudson as it flows below Trophy Point on academy grounds.

FIRST BATTLE

Bloody battles raged over these peaceful Virginia farmlands. The stone house (center) served as a field

...ospital in 1861, and again a year later, as armies fought for the strategic railroad junction at Manassas.

smoke. Congressmen had their servants spread picnic lunches in the shade of carriages and ice champagne for a victory toast. As they watched, a Union officer rode up, waving his cap. "We've whipped them on all points!" he announced—prematurely. Cheer followed cheer from the spectators in a mix of accents—German, Irish, English. The Union had yet to find a common voice.

During the fierce artillery duel on Henry Hill, Stonewall Jackson held his brigade in readiness, waiting for the crucial moment. The Union artillery kept up a pounding fire as Griffin shifted two cannons to the right to sweep his batteries. The Federals mistook an enemy detachment emerging from the woods for one of their own regiments. The Confederate line advanced silently on the Union soldiers, halted, and leveled its guns. A deafening volley tore into the battery, wounding and killing most of the gunners. "That was the last of us," Griffin later wrote.

A dense pall of smoke drifted over the carnage. Near the center of Jackson's line, Cadet Norris was about to enter the fray. For two hours the tension had mounted, and now events happened quickly. Jackson ordered his men forward against the Union forces. "Fire and give them the bayonet," he shouted, "and when you charge, yell like furies!"

The Confederate line rose from the cover of the trees and surged toward Ricketts's battery. As they caught their first sight of the enemy, a spine-chilling battle cry rose above the roar of musketry and exploding shells. The wild, shrill yell came from the throats of hundreds of soldiers rushing straight into the face of firing cannons. The cry built with a spiraling intensity that an infantryman on the receiving side said made his hair stand on end. As Stonewall's brigade advanced, the Union soldiers heard the rebel yell for the first time in the war.

Norris charged the guns, leading his company forward, when a shot struck him in the chest. The young captain fell dead as the wave of attacking Confederates drove the enemy before them. "They broke and fled like deer from the cry of wolves," noted a cavalryman watching the attack.

The top of the hill became a killing zone, changing hands repeatedly. Those who reached it couldn't hold it, finding themselves in an open field of fire. Outlined against the sky, they made clear targets for men firing rifled muskets from a few hundred feet away. The fighting rocked back and forth over the dead and dying. Riderless horses plunged and reared through the ranks as leaderless companies dissolved under heavy fire. The battle turned fluid, with the ground shaking under foot and the air pulsing with concussive shocks.

John L. Rice, a private with the Second New Hampshire, fell during the confused fighting. "In the final struggle for the Henry hill," he later wrote, "just before the stampede of the Union army, I went down with a musket ball through my lungs. My comrades bore me off in the wake of our retreating forces toward Sudley church, where our surgeons had established a hospital. In a short time, being closely pursued by the enemy and finding that I was apparently dead, they laid me under a fence and made their escape." *(continued on page 160)*

MARCHING IN FLAWLESS ranks down Pennsylvania Avenue in Washington, D.C., Union soldiers wear flashing uniforms inspired by foreign troops (opposite). Based on a Thomas Nast drawing, the painting by an unknown artist portrays the untested confidence of the northern troops in 1861. Later in the war, 180,000 black Americans fought for the North; a detail from the Shaw Monument (above) in Boston honors the black soldiers of the 54th Massachusetts Infantry Regiment.

GETTYSBURG · SHILOH ·
FREDERICKSBURG

FROM COLLISIONS OF MASSIVE ARMIES to hit-and-run raids, gray-clad Rebels fought blue-coated Yankees throughout the South and in a half dozen northern states. During the summer of 1863, a Union Army under Gen. George Meade defeated invading Confederate forces of Gen. Robert E. Lee in the bloodiest encounter of the war at Gettysburg, Pennsylvania. Fighting on the second day swirled through the Peach Orchard, seen from high above today's battlefield (opposite). Combined losses for the three-day encounter exceeded 50,000 soldiers.

Campaigning in the West during the spring of 1862, Gen. Ulysses S. Grant concentrated his forces on the Tennessee River near Shiloh Church. Confederates under Gen. Albert S. Johnston launched a surprise dawn attack on his army. The Union soldiers broke, but Grant reformed his lines along the river. His reinforced troops counterattacked the next day, winning a costly victory. A lone tree, silhouetted against the sky, guards the site of a Union field hospital at Shiloh (left, above).

Armies repeatedly clashed in the region around Fredericksburg, Virginia, midway between Washington, D.C., and Richmond. In December 1862 Maj. Gen. Ambrose E. Burnside ordered his troops to cross the Rappahannock River and attack the Confederates on heights north of town. Swept by artillery fire, the Union soldiers tried to cross 400 yards of open ground; they left behind 8,000 fallen comrades when they withdrew. The following spring a force at Fredericksburg overran Confederate defenders on Marye's Heights, focus of the earlier battle (left, below).

Swirling smoke draws Federal soldiers as they defend Cemetery Ridge during a reenactment of Pickett's

charge at Gettysburg. The bloody battle in 1863 turned the tide of war in favor of the North.

Reinforced, the entire length of the Confederate line rolled forward in a final attack. Thousands of fresh Southern troops had joined the fight and tipped the balance. One by one and squad by squad, the whole Federal force began to retreat as brigades crumbled and regiments disintegrated. Some soldiers withdrew in a rough semblance of order; others rushed headlong for the rear.

On a summer afternoon 135 years later, Edwin C. Bearss led a straggling column of Civil War buffs across Henry Hill. The former chief historian for the National Park Service guides dozens of battlefield tours each year. Ed paused before a row of smoothbore cannons marking the position of Jackson's batteries. Gesturing with a silver-tipped swagger stick, the former marine rattled off troop strengths and regimental deployments. Pacing back and forth with his eyes half closed, he drew his listeners into the events of 1861. "The broken Union army," he said, "is streaming across Bull Run towards Washington. The Confederate gunners move forward," he continued, "and unlimber on a hilltop commanding the bridge over Cub Run, a bottleneck on the Union escape route. They open fire. Boom! And a wagon turns over on the bridge, blocking all traffic, causing panic and confusion. What has started as a disorderly retreat, by dusk becomes a wild rout."

Teamsters unhitched their horses and hurried away, mounted double. Cavalry spurred through the rear units, riding down stragglers. Terrified fugitives grabbed escaping wagons or forced their way into ambulances. As the panic dissipated, the soldiers faced the humiliation of defeat. Utterly exhausted, men with powder-blackened faces dragged themselves through the night back to Washington.

On the morning after the battle, Sgt. Joseph L. Norris found his brother's body on Henry Hill and took it home to Leesburg for burial. His mother kept the gray cadet jacket, pierced with a hole from the fatal wound, and placed it in a cedar chest. That jacket, never patched, now hangs on display in the battlefield museum at Manassas.

New Hampshire infantryman John Rice regained consciousness two days after being left for dead. Swarms of flies had laid eggs in his

wounds. Unable to move, he was forced to watch the wriggling maggots. A local farmer and his wife found the young soldier barely alive. Margaret Benson stayed with him while Amos ran to the makeshift hospital for help. A surgeon made a cursory examination, but could not afford to waste time on such a hopeless case. The Bensons refused to give up. Rice could not be moved, so they erected a tent shelter over him. For ten days they cared for their enemy, bringing him food from their home and changing his bandages. In New Hampshire, unaware Rice was still alive, his family mourned his death. When the soldier had recovered enough, he was transferred to a railcar and eventually sent to prison. John Rice knew he owed his life to the Bensons and promised himself he would never forget.

The horror of the First Battle of Manassas sank in as death notices began reaching next of kin. During the fight the opposing armies lost nearly 5,000 men—killed, wounded, or captured—at the time the highest American casualties suffered in any battle. Few could imagine it was only the beginning. As the war continued, the nightmare deepened. The next year, 1862, the country would lose more than 22,000 soldiers on the same battlefield. Two weeks later at Antietam, there were nearly 23,000 casualties, the bloodiest single day in American history.

During four years of war, the armies of the North and South clashed in 76 major battles and thousands of lesser engagements.

Military actions ranged from raids involving only a few soldiers to massive confrontations. At the Battle of Shiloh in Tennessee and at Chickamauga in Georgia, the armies totaled more than 100,000 strong. In 1863 at Gettysburg, Pennsylvania, 75,000 Confederate soldiers faced a Union army of 83,000. The combined losses after three days of fighting there totaled more than 51,000 men. Beaten, the Confederate forces retreated to Virginia to face a war of attrition waged by an aggressive Union army under Ulysses S. Grant.

By a grim accounting, the Civil War eventually ended the lives of more than 620,000 American soldiers. The true cost can never be tallied. Confederate general Edward Porter Alexander, present at the earliest battle and the final surrender, lost a close friend at the Battle of Fredericksburg. Dempsey Colley was one of many to die in that action, but he can symbolize those whose names have been forgotten.

"Poor Dempsey," wrote Alexander, "he ought not to have been killed. He never cared for politics even remotely, & war ought to have let him alone. In my mind his memory recalls squirrel hunts in the old Georgia woods & midday dinners of fried chicken & biscuits by deep shady springs wherein big watermelons had been put to cool, and perhaps a little fire and some barbecued squirrel. And I love to think that ghosts are probably not forbidden in those old woods & though they may not eat watermelons, & such, any more I trust that they will have their own compensations, & with eternity on our hands I know Dempsey & I will put in some of it on Fishing Creek and Little River."

General Alexander served with the Confederate Army until the surrender at Appomattox. On April 9, 1865, he watched Gen. Robert E. Lee ride off to meet General Grant. "A great feeling of strangeness came over me," Alexander wrote. "It was as if I had suddenly died & waked up in an entirely new & different world."

LESS THAN A WEEK EARLIER, Richmond, the capital of the Confederacy, had fallen to the Union Army. The next day, Abraham Lincoln entered the ruins of the city. Escorted by a mounted troop of black soldiers, he was greeted by throngs of freed slaves. Ten days later he was dead, assassinated by actor John Wilkes Booth in the presidential box at Ford's Theatre in Washington.

Calls for revenge after the assassination generally went unheeded. The war had ended. Many of those who fought it now worked for peace and reconciliation. Former Confederate soldiers who swore allegiance to the United States received amnesty or pardons. They returned home to find a devastated South controlled by an army of occupation. They discovered plantations abandoned, factories destroyed, and families shattered. Within five years, however, all the southern states were readmitted to the Union after passing new constitutions. By abolishing

slavery and establishing the principle that the union of states was indissoluble, the war had resolved two bitter issues. And with the shift in power toward the central government, a stronger nation emerged.

In 1886 John Rice returned to Virginia. Twenty-five years after being left for dead, he rode horseback to the Manassas battlefield. He now served as the postmaster of Springfield, Massachusetts, and had come back to repay a debt. He found the house where the Bensons still lived and knocked on the door. "It would be hard to tell whether I was more pleased to see them or they to see me," he wrote.

After a cheerful reunion, the former enemies talked over old times. On his release from prison Rice returned to the Union Army and ended the war as a Lieutenant Colonel. He learned that Amos Benson had enlisted in J. E. B. Stuart's cavalry a few months after the first battle. The Confederate horseman had himself been wounded and twice taken prisoner during the war. Without realizing it, Rice had faced the man who saved his life "in a dozen desperate battles."

The Bensons guided their old enemy to the spot where they had found him near death long ago. "When I attempted to express my gratitude for what they had done for me," Rice wrote, "they seemed surprised, and modestly disclaimed all credit for obeying the simple dictates of humanity as they expressed it."

Wanting to do something to repay their kindness, he pressed them until Margaret made a suggestion. He could help pay off the debt of rebuilding Sudley Church, destroyed in the war. Rice agreed and told his story to the newspaper on returning to Springfield. So many contributions poured in that he had to request that no more be sent. The former Union officer raised the funds to "dispel the last doubt of a complete and lasting reconciliation between the North and South."

When the money arrived in Manassas, Benson hurried to tell his neighbors, who had gathered at an oyster supper to benefit the church. He read John Rice's message as tears filled the eyes of those seated before him. "There is much that we remember with pleasure," said the Confederate veteran, "and much that we cannot forget too soon."

America had survived a war with itself, leaving the legacy of a nation united. But that union came at a price—an innocence lost and finally regained. Perhaps the mending came from remembering the common bonds and, as the soldier suggested, forgetting the cost.

"Those hot, sad, wrenching times—the army volunteers, all states, or North or South;" wrote poet Walt Whitman, "the wounded, suffering, dying; the exhausting, sweating summers; marches, battles' carnage; those trenches hurriedly heaped by the corpses, thousands, mainly unknown—will the America of the future, will this vast, rich Union ever realize what itself cost back there, after all?"

BITTER CIVIL STRIFE took a personal toll on President Abraham Lincoln. A Mathew Brady photograph taken in 1860, before he assumed office, depicts a clean-shaven and confident leader (opposite). The President last sat for Alexander Gardner on April 10, 1865 (left), four days before John Wilkes Booth assassinated him at Ford's Theatre. The gaunt and weary visage of the man who struggled to achieve the "more perfect Union" mandated in the Constitution reflects the terrible cost of victory.

"THE WHOLE VALLEY was filled with smoke," remembered Two Moons, a Cheyenne who fought in the Battle of the Little Bighorn. "We circled around them, swirling like water round a stone." In June 1876 troopers of the Seventh Cavalry under Lt. Col. George A. Custer (opposite, top) attacked an encampment of 7,000 Sioux and Cheyenne. Custer had earned a reputation during the Civil War as an impetuous commander; his luck ran out on a ridge now marked by the Custer Monument in Montana (opposite, below), where warriors overwhelmed him and about 210 soldiers. Red Horse, a Lakota leader, depicted the defeat of the cavalry in pencil drawings (below).

THE END
OF AN ERA

1 8 9 0

A S SETTLERS brought changes, western Indians in 1890 turned to a doctrine called the ghost-dance religion. They danced until they saw visions of their old way of life renewed and wore ghost shirts that they believed were impervious to bullets (below). In December 1890 the ghost-dance religion and the Indian Wars ended at Wounded Knee Creek when soldiers slaughtered 200 Sioux. In a photograph taken a few weeks later Sioux tepees dot the Pine Ridge Reservation in South Dakota (opposite). Prisoners in a land once theirs, Native Americans were confined to reservations and could leave them only with permission.

CHAPTER 6
THE PROMISE OF

BY LESLIE ALLEN

NEW YORK'S NIGHT SKY BURSTS INTO BLOOM *in a Currier & Ives print celebrating the opening of the Brooklyn Bridge*

A NEW CENTURY

in 1883; an engineering masterwork, it wed gossamer grace and steely might — and Manhattan to growing suburbs.

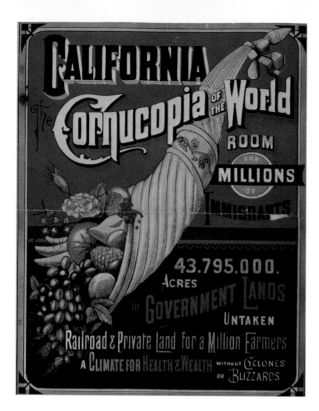

IN 1900 THE NEW CENTURY DAWNED across a land in the midst of a transformation. Millions of glowing bulbs began to fulfill Thomas Edison's promise of electric power so cheap that only the rich would burn candles. Telephones jangled. The first advertisement for an automobile appeared in a magazine in 1900. The General Electric Company built the first industrial laboratory, and a once-penniless Scottish immigrant who preached "The Gospel of Wealth" incorporated his new Carnegie Steel Company.

It was a time of mind-boggling contrasts. In 1900 skyscrapers sprouted like mushrooms in downtown Chicago, but Baltimore still counted 90,000 backyard privies. In Newport, society queen Tessie Oelrichs held a housewarming at Rosecliff, modeled after Louis XIV's pleasure palace in Versailles. Rosecliff's ballroom alone would

CALIFORNIA TOUTS its horn of plenty in an early bid for settlers (above). Before they left Europe, emigrants found themselves showered with circulars for railroads and western states. Regardless of their final destination, most turn-of-the-century newcomers began their American odysseys under New York's gateway portal — the Statue of Liberty (opposite).

have held 15 tenement apartments lifted from New York's Lower East Side; there, 330,000 residents crowded into a square mile.

The year 1900 also witnessed, among many others, these events: In New York harbor, Ellis Island's immigration depot, gutted by fire three years earlier, reopened; 2,251 immigrants were processed on the first day. A strike crippled Pennsylvania's anthracite region, idling thousands of young "breaker boys" along with their fathers. And Washington, D.C., celebrated its centennial as the capital of a nation that had become more far-flung and diverse than anyone could have imagined at the time of its founding.

In this fast-changing land, people were being remade, too. "The new American," wrote Henry Adams, "—the child of incalculable coal power, chemical power, electric power, and radiating energy, as well as of new forces yet undetermined—must be a sort of God compared with any former creation of nature."

But just who was this "new American"? With the snap of a shutter, George Eastman's new Kodak camera answered with a myriad images: millionaire and indigent, sleek urbanite and rawboned backwoodsman, Gay Nineties freewheeler and Anti-Saloon League crusader. Chances were excellent that the new American was either an immigrant or the child of immigrants. Between 1891 and 1915, the nation counted close to 17 million new arrivals, more than the total recorded for the previous 70 years. These "new" immigrants, mostly from southern and eastern Europe, came for the same reasons that earlier ones from northwestern Europe had. Famine, persecution, and landlessness pushed them out; opportunity and freedom pulled them in. Turn-of-the-century America needed immigrants more than ever to feed the insatiable hunger for labor of its factories, mines, railroads, and construction projects. The inexhaustible energy of such a huge number of immigrants, and their faith in their new homeland, did more than anything else to transform the nation.

MAYFLOWER OF A MODERN AGE, *the German liner S.S.* Patricia *bears future Americans into New York Harbor*

in 1906. Immigration's rising tide would crest the following year, when 1,285,349 newcomers arrived.

Nearly a century later, the nation that those immigrants encountered has changed beyond recognition. But the first landmarks they saw still stand in New York harbor, where most arrived. With a little imagination, visitors now can will themselves back into the world of a person seeing a place that, for many, might as well have been another planet.

Buy a ticket, climb aboard: The Babel of languages to be heard on a Circle Line cruise today is reminiscent enough of an immigrant-laden steamship. Like today's visitors, immigrants elbowed to the railing; they marveled at sights that seemed to confirm rumors of America as the land of superhuman feats. In one direction the cables of the world's longest suspension span, the new Brooklyn Bridge, reached down from the heavens like puppeteer's wire. In another rose strange, snowless "mountains," such as the 47-story Singer Tower.

Nothing could compare with the sight of the Statue of Liberty raising her lamp 305 feet above the harbor. Sculptor Frédéric-Auguste Bartholdi's colossus, unveiled in 1886, was officially the embodiment of Franco-American friendship. But the "huddled masses yearning to breathe free" made her their own long before poet Emma Lazarus' lines of tribute became a 20th-century classic. Women wept for joy, men fell on their knees, and children screamed.

Dock lines groan, a whistle shrieks, and passengers jostle into rough formation as the gangway slams into place. Here is the place of judgment, where for each newcomer in turn the gates of America will swing open or slam shut. Debarking visitors stride into Ellis Island's Main Building, now the Ellis Island National Monument Immigration Museum.

BURDEN OF EARTHLY belongings—along with bills of lading, tickets, and vaccination cards—doesn't slow the brisk pace set for immigrants entering Ellis Island's Main Building at the turn of the century (above). Most, though, had ample opportunity between inspections to cool their heels in the vast Registry Room, now restored (opposite).

Turn-of-the-century immigrants, ferried over from Manhattan's piers, often had to wait outside the overcrowded building for hours. Contemplating the nation's portal as they waited was intimidating: Red brick and gray stone trim march crisply across monumental arches, corner towers, and imposing balustrades, while eagles perched on shields glare from the facade.

The Main Building was modeled on the great railroad stations of the day, places through which tides of humanity could flow and ebb. Speed was of the essence in processing thousands of immigrants each day; "not over two minutes can be devoted to each of them," reported Commissioner William Williams.

In fact, an important part of their examination had already taken place before most immigrants were even aware of it. Lugging pots and pans, feather beds, and squalling tots, immigrants negotiated a steep staircase as the island's medical team peered down upon them. Here's one who limps. There, another gasps for breath: Heart disease? The letter

BREATH OF LIFE wafts through the dank halls of 97 Orchard Street, now New York's Lower East Side Tenement Museum. Unlikely footholds for future Americans, urban tenement flats sometimes housed dozens of residents each in the late 1800s and early 1900s.

L (for lameness) was swiftly chalked on a shawl; H (for heart) on a threadbare coat.

Visitors today climb a rebuilt staircase. At the top medical inspectors removed immigrants' hats, peeled back collars, assessed mental competence. Buttonhook-wielding "eye men" flipped up eyelids to search for the dread trachoma—a "Ct" usually spelled deportation. Altogether, about one in every five immigrants was chalk-marked and pulled out of line for further examination and, often, days of convalescence in one of Ellis Island's 15 hospital buildings.

Most immigrants, though, found themselves in an open maze of pipe-railing passageways in the vast Registry Room. Under its illuminated American flags and vaulted ceiling, 58 feet high, was space enough for many market squares, and thousands of people, all talking at once. Now empty and silent, the Registry Room was the hub of Ellis Island's immensity. There, immigrants could rehearse, one last time, answers to the staccato blast of questions (Occupation? Money on hand? Anarchist beliefs?...) they could expect to be asked.

"Free to Land": Suddenly it was over, for four of every five immigrants. The vast majority of detainees—medical and otherwise—were eventually released, too. For them, a stay at Ellis Island was a passing nightmare spent in the long refectories, the cramped dormitories, the warren of hearing rooms that are now part of the museum. One percent of most years' arrivals, though, were deported—among them the elderly, used up by a lifetime of hard work, and little children, often suffering from trachoma. In the prime of life, men suspected of being contract laborers were excluded, as were married women whose husbands, swallowed up by America, failed to fetch them. Many, if deported, could expect persecution in Europe.

Leaving the great portal to enter America was itself a bewildering affair, especially for those without a familiar face to greet them at Ellis Island. Railroad ferries took ticketed passengers to their trains, while those staying in New York caught the hourly "Battery boat." Whether they headed West or stayed East, by 1900 most newcomers did not see farming in their future. Like America's native-born, they rushed to cities. A decade later, three-quarters of the people living in New York, Chicago, Detroit, and Cleveland were either immigrants or their children.

"Every tenement house was a Plymouth Rock like ours," recalled author Michael Gold of life on New York's Lower East Side, even though sustaining the new land's promise took some doing in places so airless, fetid, crowded, and dark. Around 1900 most of the neighborhood's pilgrims were Jewish, like Gold, but the Lower

East Side has also been a foothold for Irish, Italian, German, Polish, and—more recently—Hispanic, Asian, and African newcomers.

These colorfully colliding traditions of cultural vitality make Lower East Side walking tours a lively experience. On the corner of Essex and Canal Streets, for example, the 1897 building of the *Jewish Daily Forward*, one of seven Yiddish-language dailies, now sports bold red Chinese characters and very different tenants: sweatshops on the upper floors and a Chinese evangelical church on the lower ones. Nearby, the handsome, wood-trimmed building of the old Kletzker Brotherly Aid Association does double duty as two separate funeral parlors, one Italian and one Chinese.

More Americans can follow their roots back to urban tenements than to log cabins. Just one Lower East Side tenement building, for instance, was home to some 10,000 people from at least 25 countries between 1863 and 1935, when it was closed for safety violations. The building, at 97 Orchard Street, moldered for half a century. In 1994 it reopened as the center-

piece of the Lower East Side Tenement Museum, and a National Historic Landmark. Historians and genealogists have identified more than 1,300 people who lived and worked at 97 Orchard Street over the years, along with scattered details of their daily struggles. At the age of 60, Julia Hennesy was sentenced to six months in the workhouse for public drunkenness. The Baldizzis raised their children on pittances earned in sweatshops and occasional carpentry jobs. Their apartment, along with that of another family, has been restored to look just as it did when those immigrants lived there, but even the warrens of empty rooms fill the mind with unvarnished images of the past.

NEW YEAR'S FESTIVITIES *draw tourists to the exotic world of San Francisco's Chinatown, here reflected in a period engraving. Hostility from the white majority drove Chinese immigrants, who came to California to work on railroads and toil in mines, into tight-knit urban ghettos.*

T OIL WAS AMERICA'S PRICE OF ADMISSION, but not all immigrants paid it in the cities' ethnic ghettos. Beyond burgeoning urban centers, belching stacks of steelworks and textile mills were stoked by new immigrants. And beyond the mills 100-foot-high breakers that crowned hundreds of company coal patches were themselves as many Plymouth Rocks. They bristled along the rolling hills of northeastern Pennsylvania, where three-quarters of the world's anthracite supply lay. Shiny, dense, clean-burning, and superior to the more accessible bituminous variety, anthracite was the nation's "black diamond." It powered the era's explosive industrialization, fueling industries ranging from metalworks and machine tool manufacturing to papermaking and breweries. By 1900 anthracite was the Northeast's leading domestic fuel. *(continued on page 182)*

"**U**P TO THIS TIME," remarked a Gay Nineties socialite, "for one to be worth a million of dollars was to be rated as a man of fortune, but now, bygones must be bygones." As fortunes soared, he added, "the necessities and luxuries followed suit." Newport, Rhode Island, epitomized the change.

Several servants performed the job of one; gold table settings replaced silver; orchids, the most costly flowers, bloomed throughout Bellevue Avenue mansions. Ornately gowned matrons strolled manicured lawns (above) of the Newport Casino and the Newport Country Club, where social climbing took pride of place among competitive sports.

Which summer cottage ranked as the most magnificent? Many contenders bore the stamp of architect Richard Morris Hunt, who made his Newport debut in 1888 with Ochre Court, the resort's first palace.

In the 1890s Hunt surpassed his previous opulent creations with Cornelius Vanderbilt II's colonnaded The Breakers and gilt-laden Marble House (left and opposite), built for Cornelius's brother William K. Vanderbilt, where hundreds danced at a time surrounded by golden grandeur.

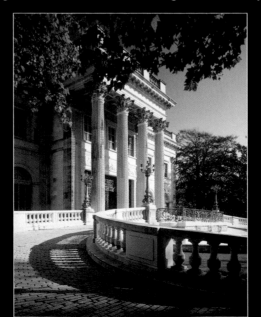

JOHN D. ROCKEFELLER

TERRACED GARDENS OF KYKUIT, ancestral home of the Rockefeller family, cling to heights above the Hudson (left). Their orderly, rational design reflects the guiding principles of patriarch John D. Rockefeller, who tended to view the business of oil refining as his own private garden. Competition meant chaos, and Rockefeller relentlessly weeded it out, forming a trust that came to control almost the entire industry. A religious man, Rockefeller defended his practices as the "working-out" of both divine and natural laws. As he told his Baptist Sunday school class: "The growth of a large business is merely a survival of the fittest.... The American Beauty rose can be produced in the splendor and fragrance which bring cheer to its beholder only by sacrificing the early buds which grow up around it." Lawyers and errand boys surround Rockefeller following his testimony in an antitrust suit (below).

GRASPING THE PROMISE of practical learning, students at Alabama's Tuskegee Institute in 1902 perform laboratory studies under the watchful eye of teacher George Washington Carver. One of the nation's leading botanists, Carver and institute founder Booker T. Washington — both born into slavery — personally inspired hundreds of African-American students in the turn-of-the-century South. Today, Tuskegee flourishes as a National Historic Site and home to an academic community of 5,000.

The industry's entire time span, from its beginnings through its decline, comes vividly to life at Eckley Miners' Village, a living museum near Hazleton. Housed in 19th-century buildings, Eckley was a company "patch" until Pennsylvania's Historical and Museum Commission acquired it in 1971. In chronological order of their arrival in the coalfields, Eckley's inhabitants moved up the economic ladder—and down Main Street's unpaved mile of 19th-century buildings, several of which are open to visitors. At one end a mine owner's elegant Gothic Revival home rises at a standoffish distance from miners' dwellings and colliery buildings; nearby, the Episcopal church where the owner's family worshiped is an inviting place of rich wood and stained glass.

Beyond, the clapboard houses are two straight rows of red—once the cheapest pigment—but the distinctions of this planned community march on. A superintendent or foreman, a mid-19th-century immigrant from England, Wales, or Germany, occupied a single-family house; farther down, the families of first-class miners or skilled colliery workers—Irishmen, by 1900—and their bachelor boarders filled to overflowing the minuscule four-room miners' double dwellings. In the even smaller, cruder frame-and-plank double dwellings of the unskilled laborers newly arrived from eastern and southern Europe, the crowding rivaled the cities' worst tenements. The tumbledown wooden breaker that looms over Eckley looks ancient, but isn't. Paramount Pictures built it in 1968 when it chose the well-preserved little company coal patch as the set for "The Molly Maguires," about violent labor unrest in anthracite country. In the 1870s the alleged "Mollies" had been sons of Erin. By the 1890s diverse groups began to make common cause against the industry's worst abuses.

In turn-of-the-century America, major strikes, often bloody, were staged against backdrops ranging from steel mills to stockyards. Railroad car magnate George Pullman hired a Chicago architect and a society landscape designer to plan his model company town on Lake Calumet. Yet the company owned everything, and Pullman's paternalism sparked smoldering bitterness among employees. In 1894 economic downturn prompted him to fire thousands and slash his remaining workers' pay—without reducing rents. The strike that followed shut down 20 railroads and paralyzed freight traffic until 14,000 federal troops broke its back.

Stigmatized for generations, Pullman is now a struggling middle-class Chicago suburb and a National Historic Landmark. The huge brick Victorian that housed the Pullman Palace Car Company's corporate offices still stands, as does the ornate Florence Hotel, named for a Pullman daughter—among many other original buildings of the visionary town that came to symbolize the era's tensions between labor and capital.

George Pullman was neither the most ruthless nor the wealthiest of the era's captains of industry. Railroads had already built vast fortunes for the Vanderbilt family, for financial buccaneer Jay Gould, and for the patrician investment banker J. Pierpont Morgan, whose crowning achievement was consolidation of the steel-and-iron industry through the purchase of Andrew Carnegie's vast holdings. While Carnegie retired—according to rumor on a daily pension of $40,000— the new U.S. Steel in 1901 became the first billion-dollar corporation. Two years earlier another gigantic holding company, Standard Oil of

New Jersey, had unified the Rockefeller family's empire. As businesses devoured each other and owner's profits grew untaxed, the old bonds of loyalty between employer and employee were fraying everywhere.

Cutthroat competition in the business world found its social equivalent in conspicuous consumption. Vanderbilts outspent Astors, and the newest rich bought their way into the company of the merely new rich. Millionaires smoked cigarettes wrapped in $100 bills, and pet monkeys traveled in private carriages. At her new, turreted Fifth Avenue chateau, Alva Vanderbilt, surrounded by live white doves, appeared as a Venetian princess to greet 1,200 guests.

Boasting far more wealth and power than most crowned heads, America's own royals needed palaces. The Paris-trained architect Richard Morris Hunt obliged them. For George Vanderbilt, one of Cornelius's grandsons, Hunt designed Biltmore, near Asheville, North Carolina, a 200-room Renaissance chateau with enough pinnacles, gables, and Gothic chimneys to rival the Blue Ridge peaks beyond it. Present-day visitors can still wander, as novelist Henry James did, through "these league-long marble halls" and peer into "alternate Gothic and Palladian cathedrals…."

Hunt's evocations of royalty transformed Newport, Rhode Island, from a quiet resort of wooden homes to a palatial fantasyland of Bellevue Avenue "cottages." Marble House, commissioned by William Vanderbilt for his wife's 39th birthday, set the pace as an architectural marriage of Versailles' Petit Trianon and the White House. Behind imposing Corinthian columns, a ten-ton steel-and-bronze doorway grille bears Louis XIV's sunburst emblem and monogram. The ballroom,

INVENTIVE MINDS TAKE *wing as one century wanes and another begins. At Kitty Hawk, North Carolina, the first airplane trembles aloft on December 17, 1903 (right); the American aircraft industry took off in the mid-1920s.*

Like the Wright Brothers, the automobile's inventors started out as bicycle mechanics. "Motor carriages" sputtered along main streets in the 1890s, but soaring sales awaited a 20th-century invention—Henry Ford's assembly line (below).

NTREPRENEURS

Graham Bell • Thomas Edison • George Eastman

Advances in mass production of the Model T lowered its cost from $850 in 1908, its first year, to $290 in 1924.

Middle-class demand sparked a host of inventions and innovations. Alexander Graham Bell's telephone (right), patented in 1876, came into common use, though in modified form. It was actually a version designed by the prolific Thomas Edison (below, right) that became the prototype of the modern telephone.

"You press the button, we do the rest," proclaimed

George Eastman (below, left), demonstrating another convenience—his new fixed-focus Kodak camera. It replaced unwieldy glass plates with film in 1888.

drenched in gold leaf and mirrors, might have dazzled the Sun King himself. Other rooms, wrapped in yellow and pink marbles, pastel ceiling paintings, rococo paneling, and delicate watered silks were, and remain, jewel boxes of European treasures in a mix of styles.

Gothic here, Louis XV there, Jacobean beyond: Many of Newport's new social elite could hardly tell the difference. European titles, as well as art treasures, could be bought. Consuelo Vanderbilt fulfilled one of her mother Alva's fondest hopes when she reluctantly married the ninth Duke of Marlborough in 1895. Just a year later, her parents were divorced. Alva soon married Oliver Hazard Perry Belmont, and moved across Bellevue Avenue to his 52-room cottage, Belcourt—designed by Hunt to resemble Louis XIII's hunting lodge at Versailles.

In fin de siècle Newport there was always something more lavish, more amazing, to raise the social stakes. By far the largest of Hunt's cottages was The Breakers, modeled on the 16th-century palazzi of Genoa's and Turin's merchant princes, and like them, graced with broad loggias and terraces. Owner Cornelius Vanderbilt II was a self-effacing man who had originally asked Hunt for a more modest villa. Somehow the architect prevailed over the Sunday school teacher. Nowadays, keen-eyed visitors wandering in the mansion's vastness might glimpse the library's imported mantelpiece, which states, in 16th-century French, "Little do I care for riches, and do not miss them; only cleverness prevails in the end."

Today, The Breakers, Marble House, Belcourt, and many other Newport cottages are museum houses. Within, visitors are often overtaken by

CATASTROPHE VISITS — and revisits — San Francisco in the spring of 1906. First, a major earthquake shakes the city to its foundations. Then fire sparked by rupturing gas lines guts the metropolitan area (opposite). The steeple of Old St. Mary's Church (top) rises above the devastation on Nob Hill. There fire destroyed the interior of another landmark, the Fairmont Hotel — since redesigned by architect Stanford White (above, left). San Francisco's twin disasters served as grim reminders that despite modernizing strides in transportation and other basic services, its great cities remained deeply vulnerable.

a dizzying sense of unreality. But middle-class Americans alive in Newport's heyday were more likely to look upon these symbols of luxury as proof of the American dream—that starting from nothing but a good idea and some pluck, great fortunes could take root in a fertile economy.

In the lifestyles of the rich, middle-class citizens saw things that they, too, were beginning to enjoy, like leisure time and places where they could enjoy it. They didn't have Newport, but they had Cape May, New Jersey (a National Historic Landmark), and, by Lake Chautauqua in upstate New York, an idyllic village devoted to concerts, classes, and spiritual pursuits. One of its most popular lectures was "Acres of Diamonds"; its subject was American opportunity.

By the end of the 19th century, middle-class Americans were flicking on electric lights, making telephone calls, and dining on fresh beef shipped across the country in refrigerator cars. Many newfangled conveniences, such as the telephone—patented by Alexander Graham Bell in 1876—had taken decades to come into common use. In the 1890s, when 234,956 new patents were granted, no one understood better than Thomas Edison the importance of turning technological advances into usable products that could ease human labor.

Edison was already world famous for the inventions that came out of his laboratory in Menlo Park, New Jersey—the phonograph, the incandescent lamp, the telephone transmitter. He hankered for a bigger, more diversified operation, however, and after his first wife, Mary, died of typhoid fever in 1884, Edison emptied *(continued on page 192)*

SKYWARD

NEW YORK CITY

REFUSING TO BE HEMMED IN by its watery boundaries, burgeoning Manhattan responded vertically. Architect Daniel H. Burnham's nearly 300-foot Flatiron Building (opposite) ranked as the world's tallest edifice upon its completion in 1902. Cass Gilbert's 792-foot Woolworth Building (right), borrowing Gothic detail from London's Houses of Parliament, took over that title in 1913 and held it until 1930, when the Chrysler Building topped a thousand feet. Increasingly, the use of new materials allowed interior space to take wing, too; it soared on steel arches and glass at Penn Station (above) and other great public venues.

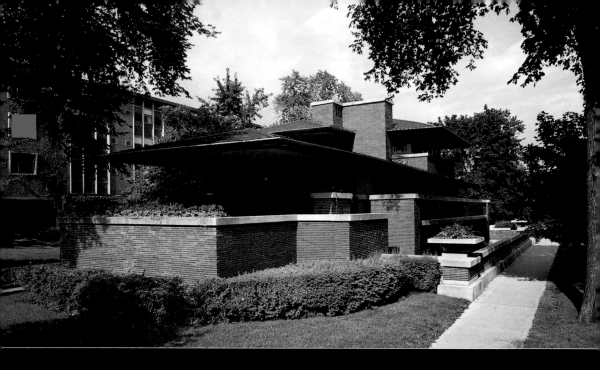

R ISING PHOENIX-LIKE from the ashes of Chicago's Great Fire of 1871, a whole new skyline—and an entirely new way of building— defined the downtown by century's end.

The steel skeleton of the 1895 Reliance Building (opposite), designed by Charles B. Atwood, went up in just two weeks. Even more remarkable than its height for its time, the Reliance's glass curtain wall inspired several generations of 20th-century sky-scraper designers.

"Form follows function," declared Louis Sullivan, the master of the early skyscraper.

Nevertheless, ornamen-tation abounded. Cast-iron grillwork frames display windows of Sullivan's Carson Pirie Scott Building (far left). Terra-cotta arabesques add exotic detail to Daniel H. Burnham and John W. Root's Rookery (left).

The Midwest's most famous architect of the time, Frank Lloyd Wright, shrugged off skyscrapers to become the champion of a homegrown "organic architecture." In Chicago's Hyde Park neighborhood the Robie House (above), still the best example of Wright's prairie-style forms, offers shade and serenity.

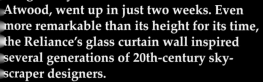

Menlo Park's large wooden buildings. Ten times larger, his new "invention factory," a complex of brick buildings in the quiet country town of West Orange, New Jersey, opened in 1887. It now comprises the Edison National Historic Site, along with nearby Glenmont, the home where Edison lived with his second wife, Mina.

Declaring that genius was "90 per cent perspiration and 10 per cent inspiration," Edison spent little time at Glenmont during periods of feverish activity. When he decided to improve his long-neglected phonograph, he recalled, "I worked over one year, twenty hours a day, Sundays and all, to get the word 'specie,' perfectly recorded and reproduced."

At West Orange, Edison, or "Don Quixote" as he once called himself, set out to invent an instrument "which does for the Eye what the phonograph does for the Ear, which is the recording and reproduction of things in motion, and in such a form as to be both cheap, practical, and convenient." In 1890 his unwieldy new kinetograph for the first time

*LOWER FALLS THUNDERS
more than 300 feet into
the Grand Canyon of the
Yellowstone River (left).
Preservation of the area
as the nation's first
national park, in 1872,
ensured that this scene
would remain unchanged,
even as a growing, land-
hungry population forged
west. Wilderness*

*visionary John Muir
wakened the American
consciousness to conser-
vation. The tireless efforts
of the bearded Scotsman
resulted in the establish-
ment of Yosemite
National Park. Muir per-
sonally introduced Presi-
dent Theodore Roosevelt
to the Yosemite wilder-
ness in 1903 (above).*

effectively recorded moving objects. In 1894 the small black kinetoscope introduced the world to the motion-picture show. The 90-second shows were made on the premises in the first motion-picture studio, a bizarre frame building covered in black tar paper and set on a pivot that allowed it to rotate with the sun. The West Orange staff nicknamed the studio Black Maria, after an old-fashioned paddy wagon. In it were filmed famous pugilists, Buffalo Bill and his Indians, New York's Gaiety Girls, a dental patient reacting to laughing gas, and many other acts. A replica of the Black Maria now stands at the site.

There were always more inventions: fluoroscopes, mimeograph machines, dynamos. In the vast main lab building alone, visitors can see some of what it took to turn the spark of invention into a prototype: machine shops, precision instruments, a 10,000-book library, and a stock-room containing, as Edison joked, "everything from an elephant's hide to the eyeballs of a United States Senator."

Edison's major inventions helped symbolize the promise of tomorrow for millions of Americans. Some 25 million visitors, in Chicago for the World's Columbian Exposition in 1893, gasped in awe as colored searchlights painted dazzling pavilions and electric fountains; they squinted and then squealed delightedly at the kinetoscope's images. Like a great feast laid out for all the senses, the era's wonders—scientific, industrial, cultural—seemed limitless, even though the nation was in the midst of a financial panic.

The exhibition to commemorate Columbus's arrival four centuries earlier was so vast that a whole new metropolis—nicknamed the White City—was built for it. Its functions ended along with the Exposition; but the gleaming arrays of classical buildings, laid out along broad axial corridors, made a lasting impression in an era of grimy industrial cities.

Chicago's White City also inspired many to think of another upcoming anniversary. Washington, though nearing its centennial as national capital, still remained a rough draft of engineer Pierre L'Enfant's vision a century earlier. L'Enfant's plan called for a mile-long mall from the Capitol to the Potomac River, but in the 1890s, the mall was a swampy pasture chopped up by railroad tracks and a depot. Only the Washington Monument, completed after decades of squabbling in 1884, seemed to stand up to the city's stature.

Visitors who now stroll down the nation's front lawn have, in many ways, Chicago's imaginary city to thank. Its three principal architects—Daniel Burnham, Charles F. McKim, and Augustus Saint-Gaudens—and landscape architect Frederick Law Olmsted in 1901 formed the congressional commission that would redefine Washington. On reclaimed land, they extended the mall and planned the Lincoln Memorial; just beyond, a new bridge over the Potomac would boldly reach out toward Robert E. Lee's family home and Arlington Cemetery. They extended southward the axis holding the White House and Monument, and along it planned a monument that became the Jefferson Memorial. Just as carefully, they planned parkland, ranging from the mall's formal reflecting pool to sinewy, 2,000-acre Rock Creek Park.

Union Station, based on the station at the Chicago exposition, was completed by 1908; the Jefferson Memorial not until 1943. Since then, more memorials and museums have risen along Washington's monumental corridors. Almost daily, celebration and demonstration, parade and protest flow through these corridors and eddy around their monuments. As the century began, the commission's plan for the nation's capital symbolized the ideal of unity in a nation still struggling to unify even as its power began to spread overseas. As the century ends, these now historic places have become islands of permanence in the turbulent flow of nationhood.

Notes on Contributors

As the author of the Society's *Liberty: The Statue and the American Dream*, LESLIE ALLEN wrote extensively about turn-of-the-century America. Formerly a National Geographic staff writer, she now reports on social history, the environment, and related topics for the *New York Times*, American Heritage, and numerous other periodicals and books.

K. M. KOSTYAL, a longtime contributor to Society publications, recently authored *Field of Battle: The Civil War Letters of Thomas Halsey*. A contributing editor to NATIONAL GEOGRAPHIC TRAVELER, she also frequently writes for the Society's guidebook series. Her *Driving Guide to Washington, D.C.*, was published in 1996.

SCOTT THYBONY grew up among the Civil War battlefields of Virginia. Scott has published books, historic guides, and articles in national magazines. A contributor to many Society publications, he is the author of *The Rockies* and *Canyon Country Parklands*. His most recent book, *Burntwater*, weaves stories from the American Southwest.

Acknowledgements

The Book Division wishes to thank the many individuals, groups, and organizations mentioned or quoted in this publication for their help and guidance.

In addition we are grateful to Robin W. Winks, Yale University, who served as general consultant; J. S. Caldwell III; Lyn Clement; Thomas Davidson; Jean-Claude Denard; Terrence Jach; Tory Taylor; and the National Park Service.

Additional Reading

The reader may wish to consult the *National Geographic Index* for related articles and books. The following titles may also be of interest.

General—James Axtell, *The European and the Indian*; Marshall Davidson, *Life in America: An Illustrated Cultural History of the United States*; National Geographic Society, *Historical Atlas of the United States*; National Geographic Society, *Visiting Our Past*; National Geographic Society, *We Americans*; Smithsonian Books, *Images of America: A Panorama of History in Photographs*; George Brown Tindall, *America: A Narrative History*.

Introduction: NATIVE AMERICANS—David S. Brose, *Ancient Art of the American Woodland Indians*; Edward S. Curtis, *The North American Indian*; Florence Curtis Graybill and Victor Boesen, *Edward Sheriff Curtis: Visions of a Vanishing Race*.

Chapter One: EXPLORATION AND SETTLEMENT—W. P. Cumming, R. A. Skelton, D. B. Quinn, *The Discovery of North America*; Charles E. Hatch, Jr., *The First Seventeen Years: Virginia 1607-1624*; Paul Hulton, *America 1585: The Complete Drawings of John White*; David Quinn, ed., *North American Discovery Circa 1000-1612*.

Chapter Two: COLONIAL LIVING—Warren M. Billings, ed., *The Old Dominion in the Seventeenth Century*; Virginia Dabney, *Virginia: The New Dominion*; Melvin B. Endy, Jr., *William Penn and Early Quakerism*; David Hackett Fischer, *Albion's Seed*; Richard J. Orsi, *The Elusive Eden: A New History of California*; Richard B. Rice, William A. Bulock, Richard I. Melvoin, *New England Outpost*.

Chapter Three: THE REVOLUTION—Charles Bahne, *Complete Guide to Boston's Freedom Trail*; Henry Steele Commager and Richard Morris, eds., *The Spirit of 'Seventy Six: The Story of the American Revolution as Told by Participants*; David Hackett Fischer, *Paul Revere's Ride*; Robert Middlekauff, *The Glorious Cause: The American Revolution, 1763-1789*; Frank Moore, *The Diary of the American Revolution*; George F. Scheer and Hugh F. Rankin,

Rebels and Redcoats; Bob Steubenraugh, *Where Freedom Grew*; Russel F. Weigley, ed., *Philadelphia: A 300-Year History*.

Chapter Four: WESTWARD EXPANSION—Bernard DeVoto, *Across the Wide Missouri*; William H. Goetzmann and William N. Goetzmann, *The West of the Imagination*; LeRoy Hafen and Ann Hafen, *Handcarts to Zion*; Aubrey Haines, *Historic Sites Along the Oregon Trail*; Merrill J. Mattes, *The Great Platte River Road*; Francis Parkman, E. N. Feltskog, ed., *The Oregon Trail*; Marvin Ross, ed., *The West of Alfred Jacob Miller*; Lillian Schlissel, *Women's Diaries of the Westward Journey*; John D. Unruh, Jr., *The Plains Across*; Richard White, *It's Your Misfortune and None of My Own*.

Chapter Five: STRUGGLE AND STRIFE—Thomas B. Allen, *The Blue and the Gray*; Paul Batty and Peter Parish, *The Divided Union*; Sarah Brash, ed., *The American Story: War Between Brothers*; William Davis, *The First Battle of Manassas*; Wilson Greene and Gary Gallagher, *National Geographic's Guide to the Civil War National Battlefield Parks*; John Hennessey, *The First Battle of Manassas*; James McPherson, *Ordeal by Fire*; James Mooney, *Ghost-Dance Religion and the Sioux Outbreak of 1890*; Stephen Oates, *To Purge This Land with Blood*; James I. Robertson, Jr., *Stonewall Jackson: The Man, the Soldier, the Legend*.

Chapter Six: THE PROMISE OF A NEW CENTURY—Leslie Allen, *Liberty: The Statue and the American Dream*; Wayne Andrews, *Architecture, Ambition, and Americans*; Thomas Gannon, *Newport Mansions*; Donald L. Miller and Richard E. Sharpless, *The Kingdom of Coal*; National Geographic Society, *Inventors and Discoverers*; John W. Reps, *The Making of Urban America: A History of City Planning in the United States*; Robert A. M. Stern, *Pride of Place: Building the American Dream*.

Stained glass in the Washington Memorial Chapel at Valley Forge depicts the Continental commander readying for battle.

Library of Congress ☐P data

Exploring America's historic places / prepared by the Book Division, National Geographic Society.
    p.   cm.
   Includes index.
   ISBN 0-7922-3652-1 (reg.). — ISBN 0-7922-4232-7 (dlx.)
   1. Historic sites—United States. 2. United States—History, Local. I. National Geographic Society (U.S.). Book Division.
E159.E9 1997
973—DC21   97-18669
                          ☐P

Composition for this book by the National Geographic Society Book Division with the assistance of the Typographic section of National Geographic Production Services, Pre-Press Division. Printed and bound by R. R. Donnelley & Sons, Willard, OH. Color separations by CMI Color Graphix, Inc., Huntingdon Valley, PA; and Phototype Color Graphics, Pennsauken, NJ. Dust jacket printed by Miken Systems, Inc., Cheektowaga, NY.